LAKE COMO TRAVEL

Unveiling Lake Como's Timeless Beauty and Elegance:Sightseeing Wonders, What to Eat, Things to Do,Itinerary for First-Timers

Regina E Todd

TABLE OF CONTENT

4.

WELCOME TO LAKE COMO

We appreciate you making Lake Como your trip location! The captivating combination of natural beauty, extensive history, and charming cities can be found in Lake Como, which is located in the gorgeous Lombardy region of Northern Italy. The tranquil waters of Lake Como are flanked by towering mountains, charming towns, and opulent mansions, promising a truly unique experience. Every traveller's heart will be captured by something about Lake Como, whether they are looking for leisure, cultural discovery, or outdoor excursions.

You will be submerged throughout your voyage in a realm of classic elegance and charm, where the past and contemporary coexist together. Explore historic cobblestone streets, take in the warm rays of the Italian sun, and indulge in the mouthwatering food of the area. You'll find a plethora of cultural riches that detail Lake Como's famous history as you tour the antique mansions, museums, and cathedrals.

If you love the outdoors, Lake Como won't let you down. Explore the area's lush woodlands, walk along the serene lakeside promenades, and take in the stunning views from hilltop lookouts. There are many water activities available, from relaxing boat excursions to exhilarating water sports, so you may fully enjoy the sparkling blue seas.

The warm welcome of the locals is equally as important as the sights and experiences, however. You will feel completely at home throughout your stay thanks to their sincere smiles and warm greetings. Spend some time chatting with the locals as you stroll around the towns and villages to learn about the local secrets that are only known to those who live here.

We urge you to adopt sustainable and ethical travel habits during your vacation. You can positively influence the area and guarantee that future generations may continue to enjoy the beauty of Lake Como by preserving the environment and supporting regional businesses and communities.

To help you make the most of your stay at Lake Como, we've created this guide. Our goal is to provide you with the knowledge and suggestions that will improve your travel experience, from planning your vacation and seeing the places to enjoying the local food and taking part in cultural activities. So be ready for this magical journey, let Lake Como's magnetism engulf you, and make treasured memories that will last a lifetime.

Greetings from Lake Como! Wishing you curiosity, pleasure, and unique experiences on your trip.

INTRODUCTION

A Brief History of Lake Como

The intriguing and lengthy history of Lake Como dates back thousands of years. The lake, which is situated in the northern Italian region of Lombardy, has long been a significant hub of culture, commerce, and tourism. An outline of Lake Como's fascinating history is provided below:

a.Ancient Origins: Lake Como's history dates back to antiquity. Before the Romans invaded the area in 196 BCE, Celtic tribes called the area home. The Romans built towns along the lake's banks, notably the town of Como, which developed into a significant hub for trade and commerce, after realizing the lake's strategic value.

b.Mediaeval era: A number of Lombard and Frankish kings had power over Lake Como during this time. With the building of churches and monasteries, Christianity's influence over the area increased. The emergence of aristocratic families and their opulent mansions started forming the cultural environment surrounding the lake.

C.Renaissance and Enlightenment:

During the Renaissance in the 15th and 16th centuries, Lake Como saw a blossoming of the arts. Rich clients who ordered exquisite mansions and gardens made the area a favorite vacation spot. Notably, it was during this time that the famed Villa d'Este in Cernobbio with its intricate tiered gardens was constructed.

Lake Como was governed by both France and Austria under Napoleon's rule in the late 18th century. The area was a part of the Austrian Kingdom of Lombardy-Venetia until the middle of the 19th century after the Congress of Vienna in 1815. During this period, Como's silk business prospered and became the main source of income for the area.

d.Italian Unification:

The Italian Risorgimento movement attempted to unite Italy as a single country in the middle of the 19th century. Several important individuals from Lake Como took part in the fight for independence, which played a crucial part in the movement. Following the Second Italian

War of Independence in 1859, Lake Como was included into the Kingdom of Italy.

Tourism in Contemporary Times: The natural splendour and rich cultural legacy of Lake Como drew a growing number of visitors in the late 19th and early 20th centuries, including international aristocrats, authors, and artists. As the lake's reputation as a vacation spot grew, celebrities and intellectuals began to use it as a refuge.

A popular vacation spot in Italy even today, Lake Como is known for its stunning scenery, stately homes, and quaint villages. It retains its historical and cultural past while embracing modernity and sustainable tourist practices, captivating visitors with its timeless attractiveness. Whether you go to Lake Como for its natural beauty, history, or culture, you will have a memorable experience that will stay with you forever.

Getting to know lake como's geography

The landscape of Lake Como is fascinating and diversified, delivering a remarkable fusion of natural elements that make it one of the most beautiful places on earth. The third-largest lake in Italy and one of the deepest in Europe is called Lake Como, and it is located in the northern Italian province of Lombardy. Here are some significant geographical features of Lake Como:

Size and Shape of Lake Como:
a.The outline of Lake Como resembles that of an inverted letter "Y," with three separate branches branching out from the centre. "Como" (southwest), "Lecco" (southeast), and "Colico" (north)
are the names of these branches.

b.About 146 square kilometres (56 square miles) is the size of the lake.

c.It is the longest lake in Italy, measuring 46 kilometres (28.6 miles) from south to north.

Surrounding Mountains:
a. The beautiful mountains that surround Lake Como provide a stunning and dramatic background. The bright blue waters of the lake and the snow-capped summits are stunningly

contrasted by the Rhaetian and Bergamo Alps, which encircle it.

b.Mount Resegone, Mount Legnone, and Mount Grona are a few of the significant mountains in the

Lake Como's Depth and Basin:

a.The greatest depth of Lake Como, which makes it one of the deepest lakes in Europe, is roughly 410 metres (1,345 ft) in certain locations.

b.During the Ice Age, glacier erosion created the lake's basin. The distinctive "U" form of the lake, as well as its steep sides and deep basin, were shaped by the glaciers' gradual march.

C.Inflow and Outflows:

a.Lake Como receives the majority of its water from the Adda River, which comes from the northeast at Colico. The lake's crystal-clear waters are a result of the river, which carries water from glaciers in the Alps.

b.The Mera River also enters Lake Como close to the village of Sorico in the lake's southwest corner.

Islands in Lake Como:
There are a number of lovely islands in Lake Como. Isola Comacina, which lies on the lake's southwest branch, is the most well-known of them all. It has a long history that dates back to Roman times and is the only island in Lake Como.

Lakeside Towns & Villages:
Several towns and villages, each with its own special charm and personality, are tucked away along the shores of Lake Como. Towns like Como, Bellagio, Varenna, Menaggio, and Tremezzo are among the most well-known.

Climate and vegetation:
a.Due to the Alps' close vicinity and the lake's temperate waters, Lake Como has a moderate climate. Warm summers and relatively moderate winters are common in the region.

13.

b.The region's visual splendour is enhanced by the rich vegetation, which includes olive groves, cypress trees, and vibrant gardens thanks to the favourable temperature. The geographical features of Lake Como are works of art created by nature, enticing visitors to explore its beaches, sail its serene waters, and take in the peace of this alluring location. Whether you are drawn to Lake Como's topography by the mountains, the lake itself, or the quaint villages, you will have a unique and wonderful experience.

Why visit Lake Como ?

There are several reasons why Lake Como should be on your travel bucket list. It is a place that seduces tourists from all over the globe. The following are some persuasive arguments for going to Lake Como:

Breathtaking Natural Beauty: Lake Como is a work of art in the natural world, encircled by imposing mountains, luxuriant vegetation, and crystal-clear waters. Visitors are in awe of the magnificent setting's splendour because of the breathtaking mountain landscape.

The lake is lined with lovely towns and villages, each of which has its own character and ambience. Every town has a unique tale to tell, from the opulent alleys of Como to the romantic charm of Bellagio and the quiet tranquillity of Varenna.

Historic and Cultural Heritage:
Lake Como is a place rich in historical and cultural heritage. Ancient Roman remains, magnificent Renaissance homes, and old churches may all be found in the neighbourhood, giving visitors an insight into the area's rich legacy.

Beautiful homes and Gardens: The lake is well-known for its luxurious homes and their beautiful gardens. A few examples of the opulent mansions that line the beaches of Lake Como include Villa del Balbianello, Villa Carlotta, and Villa Melzi.

Water activities: Lake Como provides a range of water sports to suit all interests and ages, whether you enjoy sailing, boating, kayaking, or just swimming in the cool waters.

Scenic Boat Cruises: A boat ride is one of the greatest ways to see Lake Como's natural beauty.

Hiking & Nature Trails: The surrounding mountains provide a paradise for hikers and nature lovers. Relax on the deck as you sail down the lake, passing past charming villages and taking in the spectacular view. You may immerse yourself in the area's natural beauty thanks to the many paths that lead to breath-taking views.

Culinary Delights: With its mouth watering selection of Italian cuisine, Lake Como is a food lover's heaven. The lake's restaurants and cafés provide exceptional gastronomic experiences, serving everything from fresh fish to handmade pasta and regional delicacies.

Romantic Atmosphere: For many years, couples looking for a romantic retreat have made Lake Como their go-to location. The idyllic location, quaint villages, and opulent lodgings offer the ideal atmosphere for a romantic getaway.

Celebrities & Glamour: Throughout history, Lake Como has drawn aristocracy, artists, and celebrities. Famous inhabitants and high-profile tourists have helped it maintain its glamorous aura, which adds to its attraction.

Art & Cultural Events: The area holds several art exhibits, music festivals, and cultural events all year long, providing tourists with a dynamic and educational experience. Travel that is sustainable and responsible: Because Lake Como has adopted

sustainable tourism practices: it is a great place for responsible tourists who want to protect the environment and help local communities.

Lake Como provides a unique and wonderful experience that will leave you with treasured memories to last a lifetime, from its natural beauty and cultural legacy to its leisurely pastimes and romantic ambience. Whether you want to travel for leisure, excitement, or to learn more about local cultures, Lake Como guarantees to achieve your travel aspirations in the most romantic manner.

PLANNING YOUR TRIP

Best time to visit lake como

Depending on your interests and the experience you're looking for, there is no one optimum time to visit Lake Como. Every season has its own special charm and things to offer. Here is a summary of what to anticipate during the year:

Spring(March to May)

a.It's a pleasure to visit Lake Como in the spring. As the temperature rises, blossoming flowers and lush vegetation transform the environment.

b.As a result of the great weather and few crowds on the trails, this time of year is perfect for outdoor pursuits like hiking.

C.The tourist season also starts in the spring, although it is often less congested than in the busy summer months.

Summer (June to August):

a.Lake Como draws tourists from all over the globe throughout the summer, which is the busiest travel season. The pleasant, bright weather is ideal for lakeside leisure and water sports.

b.During this period, festivals, events, and cultural activities abound in the cities and villages.

c.In peak season, keep in mind that famous tourist destinations may get congested and that lodging may cost more.

Autumn (September to November):

a. Autumn is a great season to visit Lake Como since the crowds of summer start to dissipate while the weather is still beautiful.

b.A beautiful season for touring and photography, the autumn foliage produces a spectacular tapestry of colors surrounding the lake.

c.As many traditional recipes include seasonal ingredients, this season is also a fantastic time to learn about the regional cuisine.

Winter (December to February):

a. Lake Como is at its most placid and lovely during the winter months because of the cooler temperatures.

b.The breathtaking alpine landscape and snow-capped peaks provide an enthralling background, even if certain tourist sites may have shortened hours or be closed during the winter.

c.Budget-conscious travellers may like this period since it may provide cheaper lodging costs than the high season.

Overall, your interests and the kind of experience you're looking for will determine the ideal time to visit Lake Como. Summer may be the greatest option if you enjoy more comfortable temperatures and exciting activities. However, spring and fall may be fantastic times of year if you appreciate warmer weather, fewer people, and the beauty of the changing seasons. Winter travel might be a wonderful choice for a more sedate and affordable experience. In the end, visiting Lake Como at any season of the year may be a special and charming experience.

How to reach lake como

Major cities in Italy and its neighbours are well linked to Lake Como, making it accessible by a variety of forms of transportation. Your starting point and choices will determine the most straightforward route to Lake Como. Here are a few typical routes to Lake Como:

By Air:

The following are the nearest airports to Lake Como:

a.Milan Malpensa Airport (MXP) is the most practical choice for international travellers and is situated roughly 40–60 kilometres (25–37 miles) away. To get to Lake Como from the airport, you may use a train, bus, or cab.

b.Milan Linate Airport (LIN) is another option for international travellers and is located around 70-90 kilometres (43-56 miles) from the lake.

c.Lake Como lies around 70–90 kilometres (43–56 miles) from Bergamo Orio al Serio Airport (BGY), which is well-connected to several European cities.

By Train:

a. Como San Giovanni is the primary railway station close to Lake Como. It has excellent rail connections to Milan and other significant

Italian cities, with regular trains operating all day.

b.If you're coming from Milan, you may catch a train to Como San Giovanni from Milano Centrale station. Depending on the kind of train, the trip lasts between 30 and 60 minutes.

By Car:

a.You may hire a vehicle and go by road to Lake Como if that appeals to you. Access to several cities and villages is made simple by the A9 motorway, which follows the western coast of the lake.

b.Remember that some of the roads around the lake may be curvy and narrow, so it's important to drive carefully, particularly if you're unfamiliar with the region.

By Bus:

a.Regular bus services are available to Lake Como from neighbouring cities. You may take a direct bus from Milan to Como or other lakeside cities.

b.Regional buses are another option for getting about the Lake Como region's cities and villages.

By Boat:

a.Once you've arrived in Lake Como, you may take a boat tour to explore the lake itself. You may take advantage of the picturesque splendour from the sea by taking one of the many ferries or water taxis that run between the towns.

It's critical to organise your trip depending on your preferences and starting point. Taking the rail or bus might make for a beautiful ride if you want a scenic trip and have the time. For foreign travellers, it may be quicker to fly to Milan Malpensa Airport first before boarding a train or calling a cab. Whatever route you choose, getting to Lake Como is a gratifying experience that prepares you for an unforgettable and wonderful journey.

Visa and Travel Documents

Depending on your country, the reason for your trip, and the length of your stay, you may need a visa and other travel documents to enter Lake Como, Italy. You can learn the criteria for travel documents and visas by following these basic guidelines:

Schengen Visa:

Lake Como is situated in Italy, a nation that is a part of the Schengen Area. You must apply for a Schengen Visa if you are a citizen of a nation that is not exempt from visa requirements.

The Schengen Visa enables you to travel for up to 90 days within a 180-day span inside the Schengen Area for leisure, business, or family trips.

Visa Exempt Countries:

For brief visits, citizens of a few nations, including Italy, do not need a visa to enter the

Schengen Area. It is important to review the nation-specific visa-exempt regulations for your country since the permitted length of stay might vary.

Long-Term Visas and Residence Permits: You may need to apply for a long-term visa or residence permit if you want to remain in Italy for a period of time longer than 90 days or if you have a special reason for doing so, such as to work, study, or reunite with family. Usually, these visas have distinct qualifications and procedures.

Passport Requirements:

All visitors to Lake Como must have a passport that is up to date. Verify that your passport is still valid at least three months after the date you want to leave the Schengen Zone.

Additionally, having at least two blank pages in your passport for visa stamps is advised.

Additional Supporting Documents:

You may be asked to provide supporting documentation in addition to a visa (if necessary) and a current passport, such as a trip itinerary, hotel bookings, evidence of sufficient funds to cover your stay, travel insurance, and a return ticket.

Visa Application procedure:

Depending on your nationality and the consulate or embassy you apply to, the visa application procedure may differ. The official website of the Italian embassy or consulate in your country should be consulted for information on the relevant requirements and processes.

Travel Insurance:

Having travel insurance that covers unexpected occurrences like medical crises, trip cancellations, and other unanticipated circumstances is extremely advised, even when a visa is not necessary.

Please be aware that visa and travel document requirements are subject to change, therefore before making travel arrangements, it is essential to confirm the most recent information from official sources. For information on particular visa criteria and requirements, get in touch with the Italian embassy or consulate in your nation. A comfortable and trouble-free voyage to stunning Lake Como will be made possible by properly arranging your travel papers.

ACCOMODATION OPTIONS

A variety of lodging choices are available in Lake Como to accommodate different tastes and price ranges. You may discover accommodations to fit your preferences, whether you're seeking opulent hotels with breathtaking lake views, lovely boutique inns, or inviting bed and breakfasts. Here are a few well-liked lodging choices around Lake Como:

Luxury Hotels and Resorts:

Lake Como is renowned for its opulent lodgings, many of which are old villas that have been converted into chic hotels. These hotels provide first-rate facilities, delectable dining choices, and unrivalled views of the mountains and lake.

Boutique hotels and guesthouses: These establishments provide a more individualised and private experience. These villas are ideal for a romantic trip since they often offer distinctive designs and cosy settings.

Bed and Breakfasts (B&Bs): B&Bs provide a warm and welcoming environment, individualised service, and often a sumptuous breakfast that is included in the accommodation charge. You may interact with local hosts and other travellers by staying at a B&B.

Apartments and holiday rentals: For families or groups of friends, renting a private apartment or vacation home is a great choice. It gives you more room and the opportunity to prepare your own meals, allowing you to experience local life.

Agriturismi: Farm stays that provide a distinctive rural experience may be found in the nearby countryside. These lodgings provide the chance to sample regional cuisine and get a taste of farm life.

Budget hotels and hostels: are available nearby for those on a tighter budget. These choices provide reasonable pricing and the opportunity to socialise with other travellers.

Camping: If you'd like to have a more outdoorsy experience, you may pitch a tent or leave your campervan at one of the campgrounds close to Lake Como.

Luxury Villas and Apartments: with upscale facilities and services is another option if you're looking for a high-end and exclusive experience.

As each town surrounding the lake has its own distinctive charm and attractions, location should be taken into account when selecting accommodations. Due to their convenient positions and quick access to facilities and transit, Bellagio, Varenna, and Como are preferred alternatives. However, several smaller cities and towns also provide a calmer and more tranquil atmosphere.

Remember that Lake Como is a popular vacation spot, particularly during high season. To guarantee your desired option and dates, it is advised to reserve your lodging well in advance. Wherever you stay, you will have an amazing experience thanks to Lake Como's beautiful vistas and attractive surroundings.

PACKING TIPS FOR LAKE COMO

It's important to carefully consider the temperature, activities, and regional traditions while packing for a vacation to Lake Como. The following packing advice will help you have a comfortable and pleasurable stay:

Weather Appropriate Clothing: The Mediterranean environment that Lake Como experienced has pleasant summers and mild winters. For the summer, bring breathable, lightweight attire like shorts, skirts, t-shirts, and light layering.

a.Bring a variety of clothes for the changing seasons in spring and fall, such as long-sleeved shirts, light sweaters and a jacket or raincoat.

b.Warmer layers, such as sweaters, thermal gear, and a coat, should be packed for winter since temperatures might drop, particularly in the nights.

Comfortable footwear: is an essential since Lake Como provides a lot of chances for outdoor exploration and recreation. For warmer temperatures, bring durable sandals, hiking boots or trainers.

Pack closed-toe shoes if you want to visit any old homes with ornate gardens.

Swimwear and Beach Gear: since Lake Como's crystal-clear waters are ideal for swimming, along with beach equipment. Private beaches and swimming pools are accessible from many hotels and other lodgings.

In order to protect oneself from the sun, pack a beach towel, sunscreen, and a sun hat.

Sun protection: It's important to use sunscreen with a high SPF since the sun may be quite intense, particularly in the summer. For further protection, bring a sun hat and sunglasses.

Travel Adapter and Charger: Make sure you have a travel adaptor and charger for your electronic gadgets since Italy utilizes Type C and Type F electrical outlets.

Travel Documents: Bring your current passport, any relevant visas, proof of travel insurance, and any travel-related documentation.

Create backup copies of important documents and keep them stored apart from the originals.

Insect repellent: Mosquitoes, in particular, may be a problem throughout the summer. Carry repellent to prevent bites from insects.

Lightweight Daypack: A daypack is useful for carrying necessities when strolling around cities, hiking, or going on a boat excursion.

Camera and Binoculars: Bring your camera and binoculars since Lake Como has beautiful scenery and a lot of animals. Bring a camera to record the breathtaking scenery, as well as binoculars for viewing birds or taking in the scenery.

Cash and Credits Cards: Although many establishments now accept credit cards, it's always a good idea to have some cash on hand for minor transactions or establishments that may not take cards.

Respectful Dress: When visiting any religious buildings or churches, make sure to dress modestly by covering your knees and shoulders.

Medication and First aid Kit: Bring any required drugs along with a first aid kit that has the basic necessities, such as pain relievers, bandages, and antiseptic wipes.

You may completely take in Lake Como's beauty and charm while remaining cosy and outfitted for a variety of activities by packing sensibly. Keep in mind to carry just the necessities, since you may want to bring home some trinkets and treats from this charming place.

DISCOVERING LAKE COMO'S TOWNS AND VILLAGES

Como: The gateway to lake como

Como, sometimes known as the "Gateway to Lake Como," is a picturesque city in the northern Italian region of Lombardy that is situated at the southernmost point of Lake Como. Como, the biggest city on the lake, is a thriving and active centre that provides a lovely fusion of natural beauty, history, and culture. Why Como is regarded as Lake Como's entrance is as follows:

Geographic Significance: Como is well positioned near Lake Como's southwest tip, giving it a convenient starting place for exploring the remainder of the lake and the cities and villages that surround it.

The city's position also makes it simple for visitors travelling from other regions of Italy and Europe to reach important transportation hubs, such as the Como San Giovanni Train Station and the A9 motorway.

Rich Historical Background: Como has a rich past that goes all the way back to Roman times. The city was a significant hub of trade and commerce in antiquity and was essential to the growth of the area.

Historic sites may be explored by visitors, including the Duomo di Como, a Romanesque cathedral that has striking architectural details.

Architectural Gems: The streets of Como are dotted with stunning buildings that blend neoclassical, Renaissance, and mediaeval styles. Visitors may observe the city's unique legacy by strolling through the congested streets and public spaces.

Cultural Attractions: Como is home to a number of museums, art galleries, and cultural organisations. The Tempio Voltiano honours Alessandro Volta, the creator of the electric battery, while the Silk Museum (Museo della Seta) honours the city's traditional silk industry.

Beautiful scenery: The city provides mesmerising views of the Alps and Lake Como. A walk along the lakeside promenade (lungolago), which offers breathtaking views and an opportunity to savour the tranquil waters, is a must-do activity.

Vibrant Atmosphere: its lively piazzas, lively cafés, and busy markets, Como emanates a lively and inviting vibe. The atmosphere of the city encourages tourists to get fully immersed in its inhabitants' culture and way of life.

Easy Access to Other Lake Como Destinations: Travellers may easily discover more charming cities and villages around Lake Como from Como. Como is often served by ferries that take travellers to well-known locations like Bellagio, Varenna, and Menaggio, enabling them to take relaxing boat trips between the cities.

Shopping and Cuisine: Como has great shopping options, including a variety of local boutiques, designer shops, and traditional markets. Visitors may savour regional food, which includes risotto dishes, fresh fish from the lake, and other Italian specialities.

Como is a great place to start exploring the area's natural beauty, cultural richness, and traditional Italian charm since it serves as the entrance to Lake Como. The city of Como creates the ideal environment for an unforgettable Lake Como experience, whether you decide to see the city's historical sites, take in the lakeside vistas, or go on boat excursions.

Bellagio: The pearl of lake como

Bellagio is often called the "Pearl of Lake Como," and with good cause. The triangle peninsula that splits Lake Como into its three parts has this lovely village at its tip. Bellagio has established a reputation as one of the most alluring locations on Lake Como because of its spectacular beauty, scenic setting, and rich history. Bellagio is appropriately known as the Pearl of Lake Como, and here's why:

Breathtaking Scenery: Scenery that Takes Your Breath Away Bellagio is well known for its magnificent natural beauty. Visitors are captivated by the town's scenic and romantic surroundings, which is encircled by the turquoise waters of Lake Como and set against the magnificent Alps.

Ideal Location: Bellagio's spectacular vistas from practically every aspect are made possible by its strategic placement at the junction of the lake's three forks. The village provides breathtaking views of the lake and the mountains in the area.

Historic Charms: Bellagio has a rich history, and its cobblestoned streets and alleyways are studded with grand homes and antique structures. The town's architecture is a fusion of neoclassical, Renaissance, and mediaeval designs.

Elegant homes and Gardens: Bellagio is home to a number of exquisite homes and lovely gardens that have been meticulously tended to over many years. Two notable examples that provide tourists an insight into the area's affluent history are Villa Melzi and Villa Serbelloni.

Floral Splendor: Bellagio is renowned for its verdant gardens and flower displays. The town's appeal is enhanced by the diversity of flowers and plants that thrive there thanks to the moderate temperature.

Charming Old Town: Bellagio's lovely old town, with its winding alleyways, vibrant structures, and intimate squares, is it's beating heart. A pleasant experience is taking a stroll around the old town, where there are many charming boutique stores, coffee shops, and gelaterias to discover.

Waterfront Promenade: The Bellagio's Lungolago lakeside promenade is a lovely path that offers spectacular views of the lake and surrounding mountains. It's the ideal location for leisurely strolls or relaxing by the lake while taking in the view.

Bellagio provides a wide range of cultural events, including art exhibits, musical performances, and regional festivals. Events are held all year round to honour the community's cultural history.

Romantic Ambience: Bellagio is a well-liked location for honeymoons and romantic vacations due to its lovely surroundings and attractive ambience. The town's charming environment attracts a lot of tourists.

Access to other cities: Bellagio, which is in the middle of Lake Como, offers simple access to other cities and villages. Bellagio can be reached by boat on a regular basis, which makes it a great starting point for exploring the area.

Access to nearby Towns: Bellagio is a must-visit location for tourists looking for an exceptional experience on the beaches of Lake Como because of its blend of natural beauty, cultural diversity, and romantic atmosphere

Varena: A Romantic Escape

A Romantic Escape in Varenna

It's common to hear people refer to Varenna, a charming town on Lake Como's eastern side, as a romantic retreat and a hidden treasure. Varenna emanates an alluring and personal ambiance that makes it a favourite location for couples and travellers looking for a romantic escape. This is due to its winding cobblestone alleys, vibrant residences, and breathtaking lake vistas. Here are some reasons to choose Varenna for a romantic getaway:

Charming Lakeside Setting: The lakeside setting of Varenna provides stunning views of Lake Como and the neighbouring mountains.

The beautiful surroundings and calm waves provide the ideal setting for a romantic trip.

lovely Old Town: The old town of Varenna is a lovely labyrinth of little streets and lanes that are lined with vibrant homes, flower-filled balconies, and attractive squares. Walking these charming neighbourhoods hand in hand is a romantic experience in and of itself.

Villa Monastero and Villa Cipressi: are two lovely homes in Varenna that have lovely grounds that are ideal for leisurely strolls and romantic times. Both Villa Monastero and Villa Cipressi include terraces with expansive lake views, rich vegetation, and blossoming flowers.

Lakeside Promenade: Varenna's "Lungolago di Varenna," or lakeside promenade, provides a serene stroll next to the water. Enjoy each other's company while taking in the tranquil ambiance as you watch the sunset together.

Romantic Dining: Varenna offers a variety of quaint, cosy eateries that serve delectable Italian fare. Enjoy a romantic lakeside meal by candlelight while delighting in regional cuisine and superb wines.

Boat Rides & Excursions: Enjoy a romantic boat trip on Lake Como while discovering the region's natural beauty. To tour local cities and attractions, you may either hire a private boat or sign up for a group trip.

Tranquilly & Seclusion: Varenna provides a more tranquil and isolated ambiance than other of the busier Lake Como villages, making it the perfect place for a quiet and private getaway.

Romantic Sunsets: Varenna's waterfront position offers a perfect vantage point to see the beautiful colours of the evening sky as the sun sets over the Alps. The sunsets over Lake Como are legendary.

Lakeside Cafes & Gelaterias: Take in the scenery while savouring gelato or sipping coffee at one of the lakeside cafes or gelaterias. It's the ideal approach to unwind and spend tender moments with someone.

Timeless Romance: Visitors have been enthralled by Varenna's romantic ambience for ages thanks to its timeless beauty and old-world charm. It's a spot where you and your loved one may unwind, become closer, and make priceless memories.

Couples looking for a romantic getaway will find Varenna to be the perfect place because of its cosy and romantic atmosphere and Lake Como's stunning natural beauty. Varenna offers a unique and enchanting experience for couples, regardless of whether they are commemorating an anniversary, organising a honeymoon, or just want to spend quality time together.

Menaggio: An Enchanting Lakeside Town

On the western bank of Lake Como, Menaggio is a charming lakeside village. Menaggio has gained popularity as a top Lake Como vacation spot because of its lovely ambiance, gorgeous environment, and plenty of activities. Menaggio is regarded as a dreamy and alluring lakeside village for the following reasons:

Stunning Lake Views: From Menaggio, you may enjoy breath-taking views of the Alps and Lake Como. The town's seaside promenade and picturesque vistas provide the ideal locations to take in the lake's magnificence.

Old-World Charm: With its cobblestone streets, pastel-coloured houses, and lovely squares, Menaggio's historic centre emanates old-world charm. The town's historic flavour has been retained, making it a treat to stroll around.

Piazza Garibaldi: Menaggio's main plaza, Piazza Garibaldi, is a bustling meeting spot surrounded by cafés, stores, and eateries. It's a great place to unwind, sit back, and take in the scenery.

Lakeside Promenade: A relaxing stroll along the water's edge is possible on Menaggio's lakeside promenade. Take a romantic walk while holding hands and admiring the lovely scenery as you wander with your special someone.

Villa Carlotta: Despitebeing physically situated in the nearby town of Tremezzo, Villa Carlotta is simple to get there from Menaggio. This magnificent home is a must-see destination because of its lovely gardens, elaborate sculptures, and breathtaking lake views.

Waterfront Dining: Menaggio has a number of eateries around the lakeside, making it the ideal location for a special lunch with a view. While eating wonderful Italian food, take in the tranquil view of the sea.

Outdoor Activities: Menaggio is a great home base for nature lovers. The village has chances for lakeside water activities, mountain biking, and hiking.

Golfing: Nearby Menaggio's Menaggio & Cadenabbia Golf Club is a picturesque course with sweeping views of the lake that is surrounded by thick vegetation.

Local Festivals & Events: Throughout the year, Menaggio conducts a number of festivals and events that provide a window into the town's culture and customs. The festive atmosphere of these events adds to the town's charm.

Serenity & Relaxation: Menaggio is the perfect place for anyone looking for relaxation and a slower pace of life due to its laid-back and quiet ambiance. It's the ideal location to relax and get away from the stress of daily life.

Menaggio is a hidden treasure on Lake Como because of its alluring beauty and serene surroundings. Everyone who visits Menaggio is guaranteed an exquisite and unforgettable experience, whether they want to take a walk along the lakefront, wander through its ancient alleyways, or just enjoy the peace and quiet of the lake

Tremezzo: Luxurious Lakeside Living

On the western side of Lake Como stands the opulent lakeside community of Tremezzo. On the banks of one of Italy's most beautiful lakes, Tremezzo gives a taste of sophisticated living and elegance with its rich houses, gorgeous gardens, and expensive hotels. Here are some reasons why Tremezzo is associated with opulent lakefront living:

Grand Villa and Palaces: Some of Tremezzo's most prominent villas and palaces, with their magnificent architecture and opulent interiors, are located on Lake Como. Villa Carlotta is a perfect illustration of the grandeur present in the region with its exquisite gardens and art collections.

Villa d'Este: One of the most prestigious buildings on Lake Como is the renowned Villa d'Este, a five-star luxury hotel. Villa d'Este, housed in a storied villa from the 16th century and surrounded by gorgeous grounds, provides unmatched elegance and services for discriminating visitors.

Waterfront at Tremezzo: Tremezzo's lakefront promenade provides breathtaking views of the lake and the Grigne Mountains. It's the ideal location for soaking in the beauty of the surroundings while having a leisurely walk.

Exquisite Dining: Tremezzo is home to a number of posh diners and gourmet restaurants that provide fine dining experiences. Tremezzo's eating options are likely to please foodies, from modest lakeside terraces to Michelin-starred establishments.

Exclusive Accommodations: In addition to Villa d'Este, Tremezzo has a range of opulent hotels and boutique lodgings for affluent visitors.

Private Boat excursions: Tremezzo offers a variety of luxury boat excursions and private yacht charters that let visitors explore the lake in comfort and seclusion. Many of these homes provide lakefront views and top-notch facilities. Take advantage of individualised trips to surrounding towns and attractions.

Lavish Spa Treatment: Spa facilities and wellness retreats are offered by a few of the opulent hotels in Tremezzo, allowing visitors to engage in relaxing activities and revitalising treatments in a peaceful environment.

Golf and sports: Those looking for energetic hobbies in a posh environment will find them at the adjacent Menaggio & Cadenabbia Golf Club and other sports facilities.

Boutique Shopping: Designer clothing, regional crafts, and high-end items can be found at Tremezzo's premium stores and shops.

Exclusive Events and Festival: Tremezzo organises unique events, including art exhibits, cultural performances, and music festivals, which contribute to the town's opulent and sophisticated atmosphere.

Travellers looking for an opulent lakeside experience are drawn to Tremezzo by its beauty and refinement. Tremezzo provides a lavish and wonderful escape on the banks of Lake Como, whether you wish to immerse yourself in the splendour of the ancient homes, savour gourmet food, or perhaps bask in the tranquillity of the lake.

Lecco: Embracing Nature's Beauty

On the southeast side of Lake Como, in the midst of spectacular natural beauty, lies the charming town of Lecco. Lecco, which is tucked away in the foothills of the beautiful Alps, provides the ideal fusion of pleasant city life and stunning scenery. Here's why Lecco is renowned for appreciating the beauty of nature:

Breathtaking Views of the Lake and the Mountains: Lecco has breathtaking views of Lake Como and the nearby mountains. A mesmerising scene is produced by the sight of the snow-capped hills in the distance and the crystal-clear lake in front of them.

Outdoor Recreation: For hikers and other outdoor lovers, the area surrounding Lecco is a wonderland. There are many hiking paths and nature trails that take you to beautiful vistas, waterfalls, and alpine meadows.

Monte Resegone: One of the notable mountains close to Lecco is Monte Resegone, also referred to as the "Mountain with a Saw." It is a popular location for hikers and mountaineers due to its distinctive form and difficult terrain.

Watersports and Adventure: Activities including sailing, windsurfing, and kayaking are available on Lake Como. In the nearby mountains, adventurers may attempt paragliding and rock climbing.

Piani d'Erna: Piani d'Erna is a well-liked destination for both hikers and skiers, and it is reachable from Lecco by funicular. It becomes a ski resort with slopes for all skill levels in the winter.

Abundant Greenery: Lecco is surrounded by a lot of lush vegetation and has several parks and gardens where locals and tourists may unwind in a tranquil setting.

Lakeside Promenade: Lecco is home to a wonderful lakeside promenade where visitors may stroll slowly, exercise, or just relax and take in the scenery.

Historical Landmarks: The Basilica of San Nicol and the Palazzo delle Paure, two prominent buildings that contribute to the attractiveness of the town, are examples of how Lecco's rich past is represented in its architectural legacy.

Valsassina Valley: A calm escape with charming towns, alpine meadows, and chances for horseback riding and fishing is available in the neighbouring Valsassina Valley.

Natural Parks: Lecco is adjacent to a number of natural parks, such as Parco Regionale della Grigna Settentrionale, where tourists may experience a variety of flora and animals.

Lecco is the perfect place for tourists looking for a getaway in the natural world because of its intimate ties to the environment. Lecco welcomes and celebrates the beauties of nature, whether you're trekking in the mountains, exploring the lakeshore, or just taking in the peace and quiet of the surroundings.

LAKE COMO'S CULTURAL TREASURES

Villa del Balbianello: An Iconic Movie Set

On the western bank of Lake Como, close to the town of Lenno, sits the renowned and magnificent Villa del Balbianello. This ancient and magnificent estate has achieved popularity both for its stunning architecture and for serving as a prominent movie location for a number of blockbuster films. Why Villa del Balbianello is regarded as a legendary film location is as follows:

Enchanting Location: Villa del Balbianello offers a stunning and romantic environment as it is built on a forested peninsula overlooking Lake Como. Its attractive setting has made it a popular background for filmmakers looking for beautiful vistas.

Unique Architecture: A combination of architectural styles, including rustic and romantic characteristics, can be seen in the villa's distinctive architecture. It is the ideal location for historical dramas and love stories because of its terraced gardens, loggias, and arched porticoes that contribute to its special appeal.

James Bond Movies: The Villa del Balbianello was used as the backdrop for two James Bond movies, gaining it widespread notoriety as a movie location. It appeared in "Casino Royale" (2006) and "Star Wars:

Episode II - Attack of the Clones" (2002) as the site of the hospital where James Bond (played by Daniel Craig) recovers.

Other Film Appearances: In addition to James Bond films, Villa del Balbianello has been seen in a wide range of other motion pictures, such as "A Month by the Lake" (1995), starring Vanessa Redgrave and Edward Fox, which only serves to further enhance its appeal as a filming site.

Tourist Attraction: The villa's renown from the movies has made it a well-liked destination for both tourists and fans of movies. Many people go in the footsteps of their favourite movie characters to view the mansion and its beautiful grounds.

Weddings & Events: Villa del Balbianello is a popular location for weddings and other special occasions because of its romantic setting and spectacular vistas. The attractiveness of holding festivities here is enhanced by the charm of being at a well-known movie location.

Conservation and Heritage: The Fondo Ambiente Italiano (FAI), the Italian National Trust, is in charge of managing the National Trust property Villa del Balbianello. For the enjoyment of future generations, the organisation guarantees the preservation and upkeep of this historic asset.

Due to its alluring beauty and noteworthy film past, Villa del Balbianello is a must-see location on Lake Como and a renowned movie set. The appeal of the house is guaranteed to enchant you, just as it has enchanted viewers on the big screen, whether you are a movie buff or just admire architectural and natural beauty.

Como Cathedral: Gothic Splendour

The majestic and revered Como Cathedral, sometimes referred to as the Cathedral of Santa Maria Assunta, is situated in the Italian city of Como. This magnificent cathedral, which has a striking exterior, complex features, and a breathtaking interior, is a superb example of

Gothic architecture. Here are several justifications for Como Cathedral's famed gothic splendour:

Gothic architectural masterpiece: Como Cathedral was built in the late 14th century and is a prime example of the style. Its architecture incorporates traditional Gothic characteristics including pointed arches, ribbed vaults, and towering spires.

Facade and Exterior: The cathedral's front is a stunning display of Gothic craftsmanship. The outside is embellished with elaborate stone carvings, complex sculptures, and artistic features that highlight the craftsmanship of the time.

Impressive Bell Tower: the cathedral's impressive bell tower, stands magnificently next to the main structure. It provides panoramic views of the city and the surroundings from its height of more than 70 metres.

Rose Windows: Como Cathedral's exterior is graced with a stunning rose window. The normally stone facade is given a splash of colour and beauty by this work of stained glass.

Nave and Interior: Visitors are greeted with the cathedral's breathtaking interior as they enter. Elegant columns and lofty ceilings give the broad, open nave an air of grandeur and spiritual tranquillity.

Art & Treasures: The cathedral is home to a wide variety of priceless works of art and religious artefacts, such as paintings, sculptures, and religious art. The Renaissance altarpiece "Assumption of the Virgin" by Bernardino Luini is one of the noteworthy works.

Crypt and Frescoes: A historic crypt from Roman times is located underneath the church. It has a number of historical artefacts and frescoes that provide light on the region's lengthy past.

Spiritual Importance: For generations, visitors and worshippers alike have been drawn to the Como Cathedral, a key religious hub in the area. Visitors to Como should go there because of its cultural and spiritual importance.

Restoration and Preservation: Como Cathedral has undergone several repair projects throughout the years in order to maintain its Gothic splendour. These initiatives make sure that present-day admirers may admire its architectural magnificence for years to come.

Public Events and Services: As a living example of its historical and cultural relevance, the cathedral continues to play a vital role in the neighbourhood by conducting religious services, community gatherings, and concerts.

The Gothic splendour, lengthy history, and significance as a place of worship of Como Cathedral make it a mesmerising landmark and a tribute to the earlier architectural genius. A trip through time and a chance to appreciate the creative and spiritual legacy of Italy's

Gothic period are provided by a visit to this magnificent cathedral

Silk Museum of Como: The History of Silk

The Museo della Seta di Como, sometimes referred to as the Silk Museum of Como, is an intriguing cultural centre devoted to presenting the culture and history of silk manufacture in the Italian city of Como. The museum, which is centrally located in the historic silk area, provides an enthralling tour through the long-standing heritage of silk production. The Como Silk Museum is a treasure trove of silk's past for the following reasons:

Historical Importance: Como has always been a significant hub for the manufacture of silk. This rich tradition is preserved and honoured by the Silk Museum, which chronicles the development of silk from its roots in Asia to its thriving commerce in Europe.

Artefacts and Exhibits: The museum is home to a sizable collection of objects, fabrics, and equipment linked to the manufacture of silk. Visitors may examine antique looms, implements, and machinery used during various phases of silk production.

Silk Production Process: The museum has in-depth displays that demonstrate the many steps involved in producing silk, from raising silkworms through spinning, weaving, and dying the silk strands.

The Impact of Silk on Como's Culture: Como's cultural, social, and economic life have all been significantly impacted by the manufacturing of silk. The museum emphasises how the city's identity and economy were moulded by the silk industry.

Silk Trade and Commerce: Como became a significant participant in the world silk market because of its advantageous location and burgeoning silk commerce. The museum explores the city's historical position as a major hub for silk trade on a global scale.

The Evolution of Silk Design: Como is renowned for its wonderful silk patterns and motifs. The museum has a sizable collection of silk textiles that demonstrate how design trends have changed through time.

Educational Programmes: The Silk Museum provides workshops and educational programmes that let visitors have a personal look at the silk industry. Participants may produce their own silk goods and learn about traditional silk-making methods.

Collaboration with the Fashion Industry: The museum exhibits the creative applications of silk in modern clothing and textiles via partnerships with prominent fashion businesses and designers.

Preservation of Traditional Techniques: The museum is essential to maintaining traditional silk production methods and encouraging the survival of this age-old craft.

The Silk Museum is a well-known tourist attraction that draws people from all over the globe who are fascinated by the appeal of silk and its historical importance.

The Como Silk Museum is a tribute to the city's long-standing connection to silk manufacturing and its lasting influence on the textile industry. The museum offers an immersive and fascinating experience that celebrates the art, history, and cultural significance of silk in Como via its displays and educational programmes.

Forte Montecchio Nord: World War I Heritage

On the northernmost point of Lake Como in Italy, close to the town of Colico, lies the notable World War I historical monument known as Forte Montecchio Nord. It is one of the best-preserved First World War military castles and serves as a melancholy reminder of the significant historical events that occurred in the area. Here are some reasons Forte

Montecchio Nord is an outstanding World War I memorial:

Historical Significance: During World War I, Forte Montecchio Nord was essential in defending Italy's northern frontier. It was a component of the Cadorna Line, a system of fortifications constructed to keep the Austro-Hungarian Empire from invading Italian territory.

Strategic Location: The fortification is well-placed on a hill with a view of Lake Como and the surroundings. Due to its lofty position, it was able to manage access to the Spluga Valley, a crucial route between Italy and Switzerland.

Military Architecture: The early 20th-century military architecture on display at Forte Montecchio Nord is magnificent. It is made up of a network of tunnels under the earth, as well as artillery positions and observation posts.

Artillery Positions: To protect the region from prospective enemy assaults, the stronghold is outfitted with high calibre artillery, including 149mm and 102mm cannons.

Historical Artefacts: The stronghold is home to a number of historical relics, including the uniforms, weaponry, and other gear that the troops who fought at Forte Montecchio Nord during the battle utilised.

Guided Tours: Panoramic Views From the vantage point of Forte Montecchio Nord, visitors can enjoy breathtaking panoramic views of Lake Como and the surrounding mountains, adding to the experience. Guided Tours: The fortress offers guided tours that give visitors insights into the military history, the life of the soldiers stationed there, and the defensive strategies used during World War I.

Cultural Heritage: The Italian government has designated the stronghold as a national cultural heritage monument, highlighting its importance both historically and culturally.

Educational Value: Forte Montecchio Nord is a museum that educates visitors on the trials and difficulties that troops endured during World War I, helping them to better appreciate the human cost of war.

Peaceful recollection: The stronghold now serves as a location for contemplating the value of peace and unity as well as serving as a place of peaceful recollection and contemplation on the sacrifices made during the conflict.

Forte Montecchio Nord serves as a sombre reminder of the effects of World War I on the area and is a place to remember those who gave their lives in service and to recognise the need of maintaining historical landmarks so that we may learn from the past.

NATURAL WONDERS OF LAKE COMO

The stunning scenery that surrounds Lake Como, which is known for its remarkable natural beauty, draws tourists from all over the globe. Listed below are a some of the marvels of nature that make Lake Como a genuine gem:

Majestic Mountains: The magnificent Alps, which encircle Lake Como, provide a breathtaking background of snow-capped peaks and verdant valleys. The mountains provide a beautiful location and a variety of hiking and outdoor activity options.

Crystal Clear Waters: The lake's crystal-clear waters are a marvel in and of itself. The lake's crystal-clear blue tones provide a quiet and tranquil ambiance that is ideal for water activities like boating and swimming.

Lakeside Towns and Villages: The picturesque lakeside towns and villages that line Lake Como's coastline contribute to the lake's attraction. These communities are lovely and welcoming because to the colourful homes, cobblestone streets, and charming squares.

Villa Gardens: There are several lovely homes with exquisitely designed gardens on Lake Como. The lush vegetation, blossoming flowers, and sculptures at locations like Villa Carlotta, Villa Balbianello, and Villa Monastero combine to create wonderful landscapes for tourists to explore.

Waterfalls and Streams: Numerous waterfalls and streams cascade down the slope in the region around Lake Como. The attractiveness of the area is enhanced by these natural elements, which also provide picturesque locations for rest and photography.

beautiful panoramas: Visitors may take in beautiful panoramas of Lake Como and its surrounds from a variety of sites around the lake. For photographers and wildlife lovers, the panoramic vistas are the highlight.

Bellagio Peninsula: The lake's Y-shaped design creates the gorgeous Bellagio Peninsula.

The merging branches of the lake and the nearby mountains may be seen in amazing detail from this location.

Wildlife Diversity: The Lake Como area is home to a variety of bird species, fish, and other water animals. The lake's shoreline and the adjacent wetlands are great places for birdwatchers to view a variety of species.

Natural Parks and Mountain Trails: There are several hiking paths in the area around Lake Como that take hikers to breathtaking vistas, mountain passes, and natural parks. Visitors may immerse themselves in the area's natural beauty by travelling these pathways.

Changing Seasons: The splendour of Lake Como changes as the seasons do. Each season in the area has its own beauty, from the vivacious colours of spring to the golden tones of autumn and the snow-covered vistas of winter.

Travellers looking to immerse themselves in the splendour of nature will never get tired of

Lake Como's natural beauties, which makes it a truly enchanting place. Lake Como provides a breathtaking experience of unspoiled nature, whether you want to hike through the mountains, explore the lake's shoreline, or just sit and observe the still waters.

The Alpine Ranges and Mountain Top Views

The breathtaking natural splendour of the area surrounding Lake Como is further enhanced by the Alpine ranges and mountain top vistas. The lake is flanked by numerous notable Alps peaks, providing guests with beautiful vistas and life-changing trekking adventures. The Alpine ranges and mountain top vistas are a feature of Lake Como for the following reasons:

Beautiful Peaks: Lake Como is set against the spectacular and beautiful backdrop of the Alps. For people who are exploring the area, the towering peaks, some of which reach elevations of over 2,000 metres, inspire amazement and astonishment.

Splendid Hiking Trail: The Alpine ranges provide a network of hiking paths that are suitable for hikers of all fitness levels. Hikers may explore dense woods, rocky terrains, and alpine meadows for stunning views of the lake and the surroundings.

Panoramic Views: Visitors may take in expansive views of Lake Como from the mountaintops, which show off the lake's full extent as well as the charming villages that along its coast.

Outdoor Activities: The Alpine ranges provide a variety of chances for outdoor activities, like mountain biking, rock climbing, and paragliding, which provide heart-pounding experiences among breathtaking natural settings.

Brunate Funicular: takes tourists to the hilltop hamlet of Brunate, which provides breathtaking views of the lake and the city below, close to the town of Como.

Monte Grona: A well-liked peak for hiking, Monte Grona offers a strenuous but rewarding trek with panoramic views of Mount Como and the neighbouring mountains.

Rifugio Venini: After a walk, the quiet Rifugio Venini offers a tranquil place to unwind and take in the views of the natural environment spread out below.

Winter Wonderland: The Alps that surround Lake Como transform into a winter paradise in the winter. Visitors may engage in winter activities like skiing and snowshoeing while admiring the gorgeous sight of snow-covered peaks.

Photo Opportunities: There are many possibilities to capture the grandeur of the scenery in the Alpine mountains. The shifting colours and light over the lake and mountains will serve as inspiration for photographers.

Connection to Nature: Visitors may escape the rush of everyday life and immerse themselves in the peace and magnificence of the natural world thanks to the Alpine ranges and mountain top vistas, which give a deep connection to nature.

Visitors have the opportunity to discover the area's natural treasures and take in the spectacular splendour of the Italian Alps thanks to the Alpine ranges and mountain top vistas, which are an essential component of Lake Como's attractiveness. The Alpine hills around Lake Como provide an exceptional experience for nature lovers and outdoor enthusiasts, whether they are looking for a strenuous walk, a serene retreat, or just to take in the breathtaking view.

Lakeside promenades and Gardens

Known for its stunning lakeside promenades and exquisitely planted gardens, Lake Como provides guests with a serene and gorgeous location to unwind and take in the surrounding natural beauty. Here are a some of the gardens and lakeside promenades that contribute to Lake Como's tranquil atmosphere:

The Villa Carlotta Gardens: are among the most renowned and beautiful gardens on Lake Como. They are located in Tremezzo. The gardens, which are in Tremezzo, are home to a magnificent array of blossoming flowers, historic trees, and exquisite sculptures, all of which are framed by the Grigne Mountains and the lake.

Villa Melzi Gardens: in Bellagio are a fascinating fusion of English and Italian traditions. Visitors may enjoy the tranquil atmosphere of the lake's coast while strolling along magnificent walkways covered by imposing trees.

Villa Monastero Gardens: The Villa Monastero gardens in Varenna are renowned for their botanical diversity and the wide range of plant species they include. The grounds provide a serene lakeside walk with stunning views.

Waterfront Promenade of Como: Como has a lovely waterfront promenade that runs along the lake's edge. The promenade is a well-liked location for residents and tourists to take a leisurely stroll since it is dotted with cafés, restaurants, and stores.

Menaggio's lakefront promenade: provides stunning views of Lake Como and the neighbouring Alps. It's a lovely location for a leisurely walk, a picnic, or just to soak in the tranquil atmosphere of the lake.

Varenna Lakeside Promenade: Varenna's lakeside promenade is another lovely location to unwind and admire the lake's beauty. The promenade is made more appealing by the colorful homes and beautiful.

LenLake Front and Lido di Lenno: The lakefront in the town of Lenno and the Lido di Lenno are also beautiful spots for a lakeside promenade. Visitors may relax and take in the sunlight at the beach area and well-kept garden at the neighbouring Lido di Lenno.

Bellagio Waterfront: The city of Bellagio has a lovely waterfront area that is studded with cafés and gelateria. Visitors may have gelato or coffee while taking in the breathtaking scenery while sitting by the lake.

Waterfront at Cernobbio and Parco della Chiusa: Cernobbio has a lovely waterfront promenade that runs beside the lake, and close by, the Parco della Chiusa is a magnificent park with plenty of lush vegetation that is ideal for a leisurely walk.

Lecco Lungolago: The lakeside promenade in Lecco, referred to as Lungolago, offers a tranquil haven with breathtaking views of the lake and the mountains. It's a great place for strolling, running, or just taking in the peace and quiet of the river.

Visitors have the option to get in touch with nature, admire the beauty of the area, and experience the tranquil charm that has charmed travellers for ages at Lake Como's gardens and lakeside promenades. These tranquil areas provide opportunities for relaxation and enjoyment of the natural delights that Lake Como has to offer, whether you want to wander among the lush gardens or along the lake's edge.

Isola Comacina: The Only Island of Lake Como

Italy's Lake Como is home to the tiny but historically significant island known as Isola Comacina. Isola Comacina, the lone island on Lake Como, has a special fascination for those looking to learn more about its fascinating past and attractive surroundings. Here are some reasons to visit Isola Comacina:

Historical Significance: The history of Isola Comacina, which dates back to antiquity, is intriguing. It was once a holy Celtic place and eventually developed into a fortified Roman garrison. The island has seen many different occurrences throughout the years, including conflicts and invasions.

Ruins of the Church of St. Euphemia: The Church of St. Euphemia's ruins, which date to the 11th century, are the island's most notable landmark. War-related destruction of the church in the 12th century resulted in incomplete reconstruction, leaving fascinating ruins that draw those interested in history.

Comacina Boat Museum: Located on the island, this museum displays a variety of classic wooden boats that have been utilised on Lake Como throughout the years. The museum offers information about the area's marine history.

Scenic Beauty: Isola Comacina provides breathtaking views of Lake Como and the surrounding mountains and is encircled by the lake's glistening waters. The island is a fantastic location for photography and exploring because of its natural beauty and historical remnants.

The painters' Colony: Isola Comacina has long served as a wellspring of creativity for poets, authors, and painters. It has drawn creative minds looking for seclusion and artistic inspiration because of its tranquil ambience and historical setting.

Traditional Festivals: The island celebrates a number of traditional celebrations, including the Feast of St. John (Sagra di San Giovanni), which takes place on June 24 and draws both residents and visitors for a lively display of culture and history.

Peaceful Escape: Isola Comacina provides a tranquil retreat from the busy cities in the Lake Como region. Visitors may take a leisurely stroll around the island and take in the tranquil and lovely surroundings.

Boat Excursions: Visitors may go to Isola Comacina by boat from adjacent towns, where they can also see the island's natural splendour and attractions from the sea.

Undisturbed Nature: Isola Comacina's tiny size and little development add to its allure. The island is a sanctuary for nature enthusiasts because of its rich greenery and peaceful environment.

Cultural Heritage: Isola Comacina, the lone island in Lake Como, has a unique role in the area's cultural history. Because of its historical and environmental importance, it is a must-visit location for tourists who want to take advantage of Lake Como's distinctive offers.

Isola Comacina is an intriguing location for visitors seeking to discover the undiscovered Lake Como treasures because of its blend of historical interest, natural beauty, and serene settings. Isola Comacina provides an exceptional experience in the middle of Lake Como, whether you're interested in history, looking for creative inspiration, or just wishing for a peaceful vacation.

Fiumelatte: The Shortest River in Italy

A unique and interesting natural marvel called Fiumelatte may be found close to the Italian town of Varenna on Lake Como. It is regarded as Italy's shortest river and has a unique role in the natural heritage of the area. Why Fiumelatte is a wonderful and fascinating website is as follows:

Short Length: Fiumelatte is exceedingly short, barely spanning a distance of 250 metres. Its name, "Fiumelatte," means "milk river," alluding to the water's milky-white hue, which is akin to that of milk.

Source of the River: It took researchers a long time to solve the puzzle of the river's origin. It comes from a cave located on the Grigna Mountains' highest point. A stream that leads to the lake is formed when water seeps through the rocks.

Seasonal Phenomenon: The fact that Fiumelatte is a seasonal river is one of its distinctive characteristics. When the melting snow from the mountains feeds the stream in the spring and early summer, the water flow is at its most substantial.

Geological Phenomenon: As the water rushes over the mountainous rocks, it picks up tiny limestone particles, which give the water its milky-white hue. This natural phenomena enhances the allure of the river.

Cascading Waterfall: Fiumelatte generates a lovely cascading waterfall when it approaches the cliffs close to Lake Como. Visitors love the waterfall because they can see the river plunge into the lake in a spectacular display.

Scenic Walk: From Varenna, a beautiful hiking track goes to the source of Fiumelatte. The trek is enjoyable and rewarding because of the trail's stunning views of Lake Como and the nearby Alps.

Botanical Garden: There is a botanical garden close to the Fiumelatte's source that features a variety of local plant species. For those who like the outdoors, the garden is a soothing and informative location.

Historical References: Throughout the ages, literature and historical documents have made reference to fiumelatte. Many travellers and authors who were fascinated by the river's unusual features made note of it.

Environmental Protection: Fiumelatte is recognised as a protected area due to its unique characteristics and ecological significance, assuring the preservation of this natural beauty for future generations.

Tourist Attraction: Fiumelatte is a popular destination for travellers and environment enthusiasts who are drawn to its fleeting yet alluring life. It is a well-kept secret that provides a window into the natural splendours of the Lake Como area.

Travellers who want to see Lake Como's natural beauty must visit Fiumelatte because of its distinction as the smallest river in Italy and its milky-white waters. In the heart of the Italian countryside, Fiumelatte provides a really distinctive and unforgettable experience, whether you want to climb to its source or just take in the gushing cascade.

Hiking Trails and Outdoor Activities

Numerous hiking paths and outdoor pursuits are available around Lake Como and in the area's Alpine scenery for nature lovers and thrill seekers. Here are a few of the most well-liked hiking routes and outdoor pursuits that let guests take in the area's breathtaking natural beauty:

The Wayfarer's Path, also known as **Sentiero del Viandante:** connects the villages of Abbadia Lariana and Colico and runs along Lake Como's eastern side. It travels through picturesque towns and historic buildings and provides breathtaking lake vistas.

Greenway del Lago di Como (Lake Como Greenway): From Colonno to Griante, the Lake Como Greenway is a pleasant 10-kilometre strolling path. It offers a pleasant and simple walk as it meanders past charming towns, verdant gardens, and olive groves.

Monte Brè: At the northernmost point of Lake Como, the town of Lugano is close to the popular hiking destination of Monte Brè. Panoramic views of Lake Como, Lake Lugano, and the surrounding mountains are the reward for the ascent to the peak.

Monte San Primo: Monte San Primo, which reaches a height of 1,682 metres, provides a strenuous yet rewarding trekking experience. Hikers go through woodlands and meadows on the trek, which ends with breath-taking views of Lake Como.

Grigna Settentrionale(Northern Grigna): For seasoned hikers and mountaineers, the Grigna Settentrionale (Northern Grigna) provides a difficult climb and the chance to discover the untamed splendour of the Grigne mountain range.

Water Sports: Lake Como offers a wide range of alternatives for lovers of water sports. Visitors may see the lake from a fresh viewpoint by participating in popular sports including sailing, windsurfing, kayaking, and stand-up paddleboarding.

Rock climbing: Climbers of all abilities may enjoy fantastic rock climbing chances in the hilly region around Lake Como. Rock climbing is especially well-known in the Grigne region.

Mountain Biking: The area is home to a variety of mountain bike tracks that can accommodate riders of all skill levels. On two wheels, cyclists may explore the paths, find secret places, and take in the natural beauty of the surroundings.

Paragliding: Lake Como is a perfect location for paragliding due to its towering cliffs and expansive vistas. Flying above the lake and the nearby mountains may be thrilling for adventure lovers.

Winter sports: In the winter, the Alpine areas close to Lake Como provide options for skiing, snowboarding, and snowshoeing, making for a busy and entertaining winter vacation for fans of these activities.

Visitors may explore the area's natural treasures at their own speed and take in the spectacular vistas from all angles thanks to the wide variety of hiking paths and outdoor pursuits that are available around Lake Como. Lake Como provides a plethora of chances for outdoor enthusiasts to appreciate the beauty of nature, whether they like to hike to mountain tops, participate in watersports on the lake or indulge in winter activities.

CULINARY DELIGHTS OF LAKE COMO

The cuisine of Lake Como is a beautiful fusion of regional specialities and classic Italian flavours. The area has a plethora of fresh ingredients that serve as the foundation for its delectable cuisine because of its closeness to the lake and its verdant surroundings. Here are some of Lake Como's gastronomic highlights that foodies shouldn't miss:

Risotto con Pesce Persico (Perch Risotto): is a well-known dish that highlights the delicate flavour of this freshwater fish when mixed with creamy risotto. Lake Como is well-known for its perch.

Missoltini: Missoltini are little lake fish that have been salted and sun-dried and are often served grilled with local herbs and olive oil. They are a special and delicious Lake Como treat.

Polenta e Misultini (Polenta and Missoltini): Polenta is a common ingredient in Italian cooking, and around Lake Como, it is often served with grilled missoltini on top, making for a cosy and delectable combination.

Pizzoccheri: Buckwheat pasta known as pizzoccheri is a favourite in the Valtellina area near Lake Como. A creamy sauce composed of cheese, potatoes, and cabbage is often served with it.

Agoni: Also called "agone" or "alice," agoni are tiny freshwater fish that may be found in Lake

Como. They are often served fried and are a well-liked neighbourhood snack.

Lavarello al Cartoccio (Whitefish in Cartoccio): Lavarello is another popular fish in Lake Como, and it is frequently prepared "al cartoccio," which means wrapped in parchment paper and baked with herbs and vegetables.

Prosciutto e Melone (Prosciutto and Melon): The area's pleasant climate produces delicious melons, and pairing them with premium Italian prosciutto creates light and tasty appetisers.

Gelato: Lake Como is home to a number of gelaterias that provide a broad range of flavours of the popular Italian dessert.

Tarte Tatin: Tarte Tatin is a delectable caramelised apple pastry that can be found in several eateries and bakeries all around Lake Como as an homage to the French influence in the area.

Local Wines: Because Lake Como is bordered by wine-producing areas, tourists may sample wines from the area such as Nebbiolo, Sassella, and Grumello, which go well with regional cuisine.

A superb chance to experience the genuine flavours of the area is offered by the gastronomic pleasures of Lake Como. The gourmet experience surrounding Lake Como is a great treat for food connoisseurs and a wonderful compliment to the grandeur of the Italian lakeside location. It includes fresh fish fished in the lake, mouthwatering pasta dishes, and locally made wines.

Exploring the Local Cuisine

Discovering the regional food in the area of Lake Como is a pleasant excursion that enables guests to experience the genuine tastes and culinary customs of the area. Here are some pointers and suggestions for getting the most out of the regional cuisine:

Trattorias and Ristorantes: Locate neighbourhood trattorias and ristorantes that offer traditional recipes produced using ingredients that may be found nearby. The finest of Lake Como's culinary legacy is often on offer on the menus of these family-run businesses, which frequently have a friendly and inviting ambiance.

Fish and Seafood: Due to its location on a lake, Lake Como's cuisine features a lot of fish and seafood dishes. Don't pass up the chance to sample deliciously cooked freshwater fish, such as perch, whitefish, and agoni.

Dining by the lake: There are several eateries and cafés around Lake Como that provide lakefront service, enabling you to savour your meal while admiring the lake and the mountains. It's an enjoyable experience that makes it easier to appreciate the regional food.

Try Local specialties: Be daring and sample some of the distinctive regional delicacies, such as polenta e misultin, risotto con pesce persico, and missoltini. These meals perfectly encapsulate the distinctive culinary uniqueness of Lake Como.

Agriturismi: If you're interested in eating at a functioning farm that also serves food cooked with its own fresh ingredients, look into agriturismi. You may do this to sample genuine farm-to-table cuisine and take in the rustic beauty of the area.

Wine tasting: Excellent wine-producing areas are all around Lake Como. Nebbiolo, Chiavennasca, and Valtellina Superiore are some examples of regional wines that go well with food.

Gelato and Sweet Treats: Treat yourself to some gelato, an essential component of Italian food. The greatest gelaterias may be found by exploring the streets of cities like Como, Bellagio, and Varenna. Sample the many flavours of this creamy treat.

Cooking classes and culinary tours: Take part in one of these activities to learn about the methods and ingredients used in typical Lake Como cuisine. Your appreciation for the regional food will grow as a result of this practical experience.

Seasonal Delights: Watch out for seasonal ingredients and cuisines. The cuisine of Lake Como often emphasises seasonal ingredients and specialities, giving visitors a sense of the area's year-round gastronomic variety.

Visit Local Markets: Look around your neighbourhood's markets and food stands to find specialty cheeses, cured meats, fresh produce and other locally produced goods. These markets provide the opportunity to taste and buy real regional specialties.

Discovering the regional food in and around Lake Como is not only a great culinary experience, but also a chance to engage with the area's rich cultural legacy. Lake Como's culinary options are certain to make a lasting effect on your taste buds and create priceless memories of your stay by the lake, from lakefront dining to family-run trattorias and fresh seafood meals.

Must try Dishes and Delicacies

There are a number of must-try foods and treats that highlight the area's distinctive flavours and culinary traditions while sampling the regional cuisine in and around Lake Como.

Here are some foods and treats you shouldn't miss while you're there:

Risotto con Pesce Persico (Perch Risotto): Creamy risotto prepared with perch, a plentiful freshwater fish in Lake Como, which is locally fished. The thick and savoury rice pairs nicely with the delicate flavour of the fish.

Missoltini: Agoni fish that has been sun-dried and salted; a Lake Como speciality. Usually grilled with olive oil and regional spices, these little fish make an interesting and savoury snack.

Polenta e Misultin (Polenta and Missoltini): is a dish that combines grilled missoltini with soft, creamy polenta for a hearty and delectable flavour combination.

Pizzoccheri: A meal of buckwheat pasta prepared with potatoes, cabbage, and plenty of melted cheese. It is an authentic Valtellina speciality that is filling and hearty.

Whitefish: prepared "al cartoccio," wrapped in parchment paper and baked with herbs and vegetables, is known as Lavarello al Cartoccio (Whitefish in Cartoccio). This cooking method preserves the fish's moisture and enables the flavours to mingle.

Ossobuco alla Milanese: Although not exclusive to Lake Como, you can often find this Milanese delicacy at eateries along the lake. It includes braised veal shanks that are served with a lemon, garlic, and parsley gremolata.

Tremezzina style Tarts: These tarts, a Tremezzo dessert speciality, have a shortcrust pastry shell that is filled with almonds, sugar and egg whites to make a delectable delicacy.

Local Cheeses: Try local cheeses like the silky goat milk cheese Scimudin and the classic Alpine cheese Bitto. For a delicious flavor, serve these cheeses with honey or regional preserves.

Gelato: Indulge in some real Italian gelato, which comes in a variety of flavours and is each a creamy and energising pleasure.

Local wines: Wine-producing areas around Lake Como. To fully experience the rich wine culture of the region, try some of the regional wines, such as Nebbiolo, Sassella, and Grumello.

These must-try foods and specialties will expose you to the area's distinctive flavours and culinary traditions as you discover the gastronomic wonders of Lake Como. Each mouthful will be a lovely and unforgettable experience, from delectable desserts and local wines to fresh seafood and pasta entrees. Happy eating!

Lakefront Dining With a View

A classic Lake Como experience is lakefront eating with a view. Along the lake's banks, the area is home to a large number of eateries and cafés that provide breathtaking views of the lake's glistening waters and the surrounding mountains. Here are some excellent locations for lakeside dining with stunning views:

Bellagio: is well known for its quaint waterfront promenade dotted with eateries and cafés. When dining here, you can see the whole lake, including Lake Como's fusing branches.

Varenna: There are a number of lakeside restaurants with terraces in this charming town. Enjoy a dinner while taking in the peaceful surroundings and the colourful homes.

Como Waterfront: The waterfront of the city of Como is a bustling location with eateries and cafés that provide lovely views of the lake. It's a wonderful place to unwind and watch the boats go past.

Lenno: The lakefront area in the town of Lenno is attractive and ideal for lakeside eating. As you eat, see the lovely Comacina Island and the lake's western branch.

Tremezzo: Tremezzo is the location of a number of opulent hotels and eateries that provide lakefront dining with breathtaking views of the lake and the renowned Villa Carlotta gardens.

Cernobbio: Cernobbio's lakeside promenade is lined with eateries and cafés, making it a picturesque location to enjoy your dinner while gazing out over the lake and the quaint town.

Menaggio: There are several eating establishments with views of the lake and the surrounding mountains along Menaggio's lakefront promenade. A supper around sunset is the ideal time to eat there.

Lecco: The Lungolago (lakefront) of Lecco is home to a number of eateries and pubs where patrons may savour delectable cuisine while admiring the eastern arm of Lake Como.

Villa d'Este, Cernobbio: The beautiful lakeside dining experience is offered by the storied luxury hotel, Villa d'Este. Enjoy fine dining while being surrounded by the stunning grounds and lake of the hotel.

Il Gatto Nero in Cernobbio: is a well-known eatery with a lovely patio that looks out over the lake. It is well known for its delectable Italian food and seafood delicacies.

Visiting Local Markets and Food Festivals

A lovely way to enjoy the thriving culinary scene and fully immerse yourself in the community surrounding Lake Como is to visit local markets and food festivals. These events provide an opportunity to try genuine cuisine, local goods, and local farmers and craftsmen. Here are some tips for visiting regional markets and cuisine events in the Lake Como region:

Local Markets

Como Market (Mercato di Como): Every Tuesday and Thursday morning, the city of Como has a bustling market at Piazza Vittoria. A wide range of fresh fruit, regional cheeses, cured meats, and handcrafted goods are available here.

Bellagio Market (Mercato di Bellagio): Every Thursday morning, a market is held in Bellagio along the lakefront promenade. Explore the vendors and find regional treats and crafts.

The Varenna Market (Mercato di Varenna): is a weekly event that takes place at Piazza San Giorgio every Wednesday. It provides an opportunity to sample regional goods and speak with welcoming sellers.

Lenno Market: Every Tuesday, Lenno has a market along the lakeside known as the Mercato di Lenno. Look through the vendors offering local specialities and fresh produce.

Lecco Market: Every Wednesday morning, the Lecco Market (Mercato di Lecco) is held at Piazza XX Settembre and features a wide range of regional foods and goods.

Food Festivals.

Sagra di San Giovanni: On June 24th, villages around Lake Como celebrate this festival in honour of Saint John the Baptist. There are food booths, live music, and other activities. It's a wonderful chance to sample regional cuisine and take part in cultural festivities.

Sagra dei Crotti (Chiavenna): Although not located immediately on Lake Como, the Sagra dei Crotti is held in September in the neighbouring town of Chiavenna. It honours regional cuisine and wine customs, including tasting events held in age-old mountain caves known as "crotti."

Sagra della Rana (Como): The Sagra della Rana (Frog Festival) is a jovial event that takes place in Como in October and features a variety of frog-themed foods, including frog legs, risotto, and spaghetti.

Palio Del Baradello: Como celebrates the Palio del Baradello in September, a festival with a mediaeval theme that includes historical reenactments, street entertainers, and food stands selling regional cuisine.

Festa della Madonna Ghisallo: Even though it isn't exactly a culinary festival, the Festa della Madonna del Ghisallo in Magreglio is a well-liked occasion for bikers. It includes a pilgrimage and the opportunity to sample regional food.

You may learn about Lake Como's regional cuisines and culinary traditions by going to local markets and food festivals. It's a great opportunity to get involved with the community, help small producers, and preserve the memories of your culinary adventure through this alluring area.

WATER ACTIVITIES AND WATERFRONT LEISURE

Lake Como sailing and boating

An outstanding approach to discover the stunning beauty of the lake and its surroundings is by sailing and boating on Lake Como. For sailing enthusiasts and those looking for an unforgettable time on the sea, the picturesque surroundings and crystal-clear waters provide for the ideal backdrop. Here are some excellent choices for boating and sailing on Lake Como:

Boat Tours: Explore Lake Como's attractions, including its quaint villages, antique homes, and stunning scenery, by taking a guided boat excursion. Popular locations including Bellagio, Varenna, and Villa del Balbianello are often visited on boat cruises.

Private Boat Rental: To explore the lake at your own leisure, rent a private boat or hire a local captain. This gives you the opportunity to choose your own itinerary, giving you a more tailored experience.

Sailing: Lake Como is a great place to go sailing due to its calm seas and consistent breezes. To experience the excitement of sailing across the lake, you may either rent a sailboat or sign up for a sailing expedition.

Motor Boat Rentals: Rent a motorboat to freely explore the lake and find isolated beaches, secret coves, and quaint settlements.

Stand-Up Paddleboarding and Kayaking:
If you want a more active and private experience on the water, try stand-up paddleboarding or kayaking. Paddle around the shoreline to see the natural splendour firsthand.

Ferry Rides: Benefit from the many ferries that link the villages surrounding Lake Como. It's a convenient and beautiful method to go from one place to another while taking in the scenery from the sea.

Sunset Cruises: Treat yourself to a romantic evening tour on the lake, which several boat companies provide as a way to see the mesmerising sunset over the water.

Villa Visits by Boat: Villa Balbianello and Villa Carlotta are two well-known homes on Lake Como that may be reached by boat. Visit these storied and stunning sites while taking a boat cruise.

Fishing Trips: Join a fishing excursion with a local guide to learn about traditional fishing methods and catch fish on the lake.

Watersports Centers: Some lakeside communities include water sports facilities that provide a range of water-based adventures, including water skiing, wakeboarding, and tube rides.

Sailing and boating on Lake Como provide a unique viewpoint of the area's architectural marvels and natural beauties. The lake provides a variety of activities that appeal to various interests and tastes, whether you choose a leisurely boat trip, an intense sailing excursion, or a tranquil paddle along the coast.

Windsurfing and Kitesurfing

Due to the lake's good wind conditions and picturesque surroundings, the exciting water sports activities of windsurfing and kitesurfing are quite common in the Lake Como area. Both activities provide an exhilarating experience and a unique opportunity to take in the lake's natural beauty. The following information will help you windsurf and kitesurf in Lake Como:

Windsurfing on Lake Como:

a.A person who is windsurfing stands on a board while holding onto a sail that is connected to a mast, combining features of sailing and surfing.

b.The geology of Lake Como and its wind patterns are perfect for windsurfing, especially in the summer when the "Breva" wind comes from the south in the afternoons.

c.Around the lake, there are a number of windsurfing schools and rental businesses that provide gear for riders of all skill levels, from absolute beginners to experts.

d.On the northern end of the lake, where the wind is stronger and more reliable, are Domaso, Gravedona, and Colico, which are well-liked windsurfing locations.

Kitesurfing on Lake Como:

a.Riding a tiny surfboard or a kiteboard while being driven by a big kite that captures the wind is known as kitesurfing, sometimes known as kiteboarding.

b.The "Tivano," a thermally produced afternoon breeze off Lake Como, creates ideal conditions for kiteboarding in the summer.

c.While kitesurfing is popular in the centre and southern portions of the lake, where the wind is more consistent, windsurfing is more common on the northern end of the lake.

d.Towns like Cernobbio, Dervio, and Colico provide kitesurfing schools and rental facilities that provide instruction and gear for both novice and expert kitesurfers.

Safety Advice for Kite and Windsurfing

a.Before going out on the lake, always check the weather and wind predictions.

b.Wear the proper safety equipment, such as a harness and a life jacket (for kiteboarding).

c.If you're a newbie, take classes to acquire basic skills and safety precautions.

d.Be considerate to other water users and watch out for other boats on the lake.

e.Be mindful of any water sports-related municipal laws or limitations.

Both windsurfing and kitesurfing provide a fun opportunity to enjoy Lake Como's natural beauty while using the force of the wind. No matter whether you're an experienced windsurfer or a kitesurfer for the first time, Lake Como's crystal-clear waters and breathtaking scenery provide for an unbeatable environment for these exhilarating water sports.

Swimming in Waters of Perfect Clarity

It is energising and invigorating to swim in Lake Como's crystal-clear waters. The lake is a popular destination for water enthusiasts because of its crystal-clear waters, which are also noted for their cleanliness. What you should know before swimming in Lake Como's pristine waters is as follows:

Water Quality: The water in Lake Como is of the highest quality and continuously upholds strict requirements of cleanliness. Numerous mountain streams and rivers feed the lake, guaranteeing a steady supply of fresh water.

Safety: While swimming in Lake Como is typically safe, it's important to use care and follow safety precautions. Consider swimming only in approved locations while keeping an eye out for boats and underwater currents.

Public Beaches: There are public beaches with designated swimming areas in several of the municipalities around Lake Como. During the busiest times of the year, these beaches often include amenities including toilets, changing rooms, and lifeguards.

Lidos: Lidos are well-liked places that provide access to lakes along with extras like sun loungers, umbrellas, bars, and restaurants. They provide a cosy and relaxing setting for swimming and unwinding.

Private Beaches: A few hotels and resorts provide their guests exclusive access to their own private beaches. You may swim in more quiet and peaceful surroundings if you stay at one of these lodgings.

Rocky coasts: Lake Como has various rocky coasts, which enhance the beauty of the surroundings. When entering the lake, be careful to put on suitable water shoes to protect your feet from rocks and stones.

Water Temperature: Throughout the year, Lake Como's water temperature changes. The summer months, from June through September, when temperatures are warmer, are often the most pleasant for swimming.

Early Mornings: To enjoy the lake in a more tranquil and quiet setting before the masses come, consider swimming in the early morning.

Sunset Swims: If you want a surreal swimming experience, go for a swim at sunset. An air of wonder permeates the area as the sun sets over the lake.

Water sports: In addition to swimming, Lake Como provides kayaking, paddleboarding, and snorkelling so that you may see the lake's splendour from a variety of angles.

Swimming in Lake Como's crystal-clear waters is a wonderful experience that lets you fully appreciate this gorgeous lake's natural splendour. The crystal-clear and welcoming waters of Lake Como provide a lovely vacation and an opportunity to reconnect with nature, whether you prefer to swim in authorised areas, relax at a lido, or explore quiet coves.

Lakeside Relaxation and Sunbathing

The ideal way to unwind, enjoy the sun, and take in the gorgeous surroundings is to lounge by the lake and sunbathe on Lake Como. The pure waters and breathtaking scenery of Lake Como provide a number of lovely locations for relaxing and sunbathing. Here's how to get the most out of your time relaxing by the lake:

Public Beaches: There are dedicated sunbathing spots at public beaches or lidos in several of the municipalities that surround Lake Como. These locations often include amenities like umbrellas, loungers, and neighbouring cafés or restaurants.

Private Beaches and Resorts: A few hotels and resorts provide their customers exclusive access to their own private beaches. You may take advantage of a more quiet and serene sunbathing experience by booking one of these lodgings.

Lakes and Parks: Many lakefront parks and promenades can be found in the towns around the lake, where you may lay out a towel, relax on the grass, and take in the scenery while soaking up the rays.

Sunbathing on Boat Tours: If you're taking a boat trip on the lake, many of the boats have open decks where you may unwind and tan while soaking in the fresh air and beautiful scenery.

Villa Gardens: Some venerable homes around Lake Como, including Villa Carlotta and Villa del Balbianello, feature impeccably kept grounds where you may unwind and sunbathe in a peaceful environment.

SunScreen: Remember to use sunscreen and protect your skin from the sun's rays, particularly during the sun's peak hours. For further protection, bring a hat, sunglasses, and a cover-up for the beach.

Cooling off in the Lake: Get cool during your sunbathing periods by taking ice-cold dives in the lake. Lake Como's crystal-clear waters are welcoming and ideal for a leisurely dip.

Lakeside Picnic: Bring a picnic and have a tranquil supper by the lake. Many public spaces and parks include grassy areas or picnic tables where you may have a delicious dinner by the lake.

Sunrise and Sunset: Consider lying out in the sun in the early morning or late afternoon to take in the serene beauty of the dawn or the sunset over the lake.

Unplug & Reconnect with Nature: Take advantage of this lakeside downtime to disconnect from technology, savour the serenity of nature, and re-establish a connection with Lake Como's serene surroundings.

On Lake Como, sunbathing and relaxing by the water provide a restorative experience among the breathtaking natural surroundings. The tranquil atmosphere of Lake Como makes for the ideal background for a leisurely and sun-drenched getaway, whether you want to relax on a beach, sprawl out in a park, or take advantage of the luxuries of a private resort.

OFF THE BEATEN PATH

Going off the main road may be a rewarding experience for those hoping to discover the hidden treasures and lesser-known sights around Lake Como. Consider these off-the-beaten-path locations and activities when planning your trip:

Lake Piano and Pian di Spagna Nature Reserve: A tiny but charming lake surrounded by marshes and reed beds, Lake Piano is situated on the northernmost point of Lake Como. A sanctuary for birding and nature treks is the neighbouring Pian di Spagna Nature Reserve.

Monte Grona Hike: If you're looking for a difficult yet rewarding journey, think about climbing Monte Grona. Beautiful panoramic views of Lake Como and the neighbouring Alps are available from this lesser-known hike.

San Martino Church: While many tourists go to the opulent houses and gardens, San Martino Church in Griante provides a more sedate and private experience. The church offers a peaceful setting and lovely paintings.

Orrido di Bellano: The town of Bellano is home to the natural canyon and waterfall known as Orrido di Bellano. Experience the strength and beauty of this hidden gem by strolling along the hanging walkways.

Castello di Vezio: Varenna is a well-known tourist site, but the Castello di Vezio, a mediaeval castle set on a hill, offers a more private and historical attraction with stunning lake views.

The Village of Corenno Plinio: This little, endearing community on the eastern bank of Lake Como provides a window into country life in Italy. Take a stroll around the city's little lanes and take in the historic architecture.

Boat Trips to Comacina Island: The lone island in Lake Como, Comacina Island, is often disregarded by visitors. Visit the island by boat to see the archeological remains and take in the peaceful atmosphere.

Pigra: A cable car may take you from Argegno to the settlement of Pigra, which is positioned high above Lake Como. Without the tourists, it provides breathtaking views of the lake and the mountains in the area.

Menaggio's Museum of Navigational Instruments: is a hidden treasure despite the fact that Menaggio is a well-known tourist destination. Find out about the lake's maritime past while exploring a fascinating collection of navigational aids.

Piona Abbey: is a quiet, less-frequented monastic monastery with lovely grounds and a tranquil lakeside location. It is situated on the eastern bank of Lake Como.

You may explore Lake Como's surrounding areas' lesser-known gems and really experience their rustic appeal by going off the main path. Accept the need to explore, and you'll be rewarded with unusual encounters and peaceful times away from the masses.

Hidden Gems

Como.There are many undiscovered attractions around Lake Como that provide a feeling of discovery and an opportunity to get away from the masses. These lesser-known locations and attractions provide a distinctive and genuine view of the area. Here are a few intriguing local attractions around Lake Como:

Laghetto di Piona (Small Lake of Piona): This quiet lake, which is close to the Piona Abbey, provides a calm environment for a leisurely stroll or a quiet period of thought.

Lierna and the Olcio Peninsula: The Olcio Peninsula is a hidden treasure in Lierna, a beautiful community with a gorgeous shoreline and a peaceful beach away from the tourists.

Valchiavenna: is a magnificent alpine valley located north of Lake Como and is renowned for its gorgeous landscape, charming towns, and delectable regional food.

Bellano Ravine (Orrido di Bellano):a magnificent ravine with gushing waterfalls and striking rock formations. Visitors may get a close-up view of this undiscovered gem thanks to walkways and bridges.

San Benedetto Hermitage: also known as Eremo di San Benedetto, is a remote hermitage built on a rock above Lake Como. It requires a trek to get there, but the breathtaking sights and peaceful atmosphere are definitely worth it.

Spina Verde Regional Park: Located just north of Como, Spina Verde Regional Park has stunning lake views, hiking paths, and scenic lookout spots. For those who like the outdoors and the natural world, it's a great location.

The Moltrasio Balcony: is a picturesque lookout point that is situated above the village of Moltrasio. It provides sweeping views of the region, including Lake Como.

Grotte del Rescia (Rescia caverns): A short distance from Lake Como, the Rescia Caves are a network of stalactite and stalagmite-filled caverns.

Pescalo Bay: Although Bellagio is well-known, its lovely Pescallo Bay is sometimes overlooked. This little fishing community provides a serene and beautiful ambiance.

Fiumelatte Trail: Take a stroll along this trail that follows Italy's smallest river, the Fiumelatte River, as it empties into Lake Como close to Varenna.

You may discover more about the splendour and serenity of Lake Como and its surroundings by exploring these hidden jewels. These less well-known locations provide a feeling of adventure and a chance to engage with the environment and local culture in a more direct and sincere manner.

Day Trips

The central position of Lake Como in Northern Italy makes it a great starting point for day excursions to neighbouring locations, enabling you to explore more of the area and take in a variety of sights. From Lake Como, consider the following fascinating day trip options:

Milan: a cosmopolitan city renowned for its fashion, art, and historical sites. Visit the beautiful Duomo di Milano, take in Leonardo da Vinci's "The Last Supper" at Santa Maria delle Grazie, and wander around Galleria Vittorio Emanuele II, Milan's premium retail zone.

Bergamo: Visit Bergamo, a gorgeous city with a quaint upper town from the mediaeval era (Città Alta) and a contemporary lower town (Città Bassa). Explore historic squares and cathedrals while taking in the spectacular views from the old city walls.

Lugano(Switzerland): Drive a short distance to Lugano, Switzerland, which is tucked away in the Swiss Alps. Experience Swiss culture and food while strolling along the opulent lakefront promenade and stopping at Parco Ciani.

Valtellina wine Region: which is north of Lake Como, by taking a wine tour. Sample top-notch regional wines like Nebbiolo and Chiavennasca while taking in the beautiful vineyard scenery.

St. Moritz, Switzerland: Visit St. Moritz in Switzerland for a more exciting day vacation. When it snows, engage in winter sports or see the breathtaking Engadin Valley and glacial Lake St. Moritz.

Lake Maggiore: the second-largest lake in Italy. Take a boat journey to the lovely village of Stresa, tour the grounds of Villa Taranto, and visit the Borromean Islands.

Como Brunate Funicular:is a lovely hilltop town with expansive views of Lake Como and the surrounding mountains. It is accessible by funicular from Como. Take a leisurely walk while admiring the stunning environment.

Lake Lugano Boat Tour: Experience a lovely boat cruise on Lake Lugano while discovering the lake's alluring shores and charming settlements.

Bellinzona: Switzerland, a UNESCO World Heritage site renowned for its magnificent mediaeval castles.

Adda River region and see Leonardo da Vinci's ferry: which is still in use today. Enjoy the sights of the river while travelling on the old boat.

These days, excursions from Lake Como provide a variety of experiences, including discovering energetic towns and appreciating the local natural and cultural history. Your whole experience in this alluring area of Italy is enhanced by each destination's unique character.

Valsassina: A Mountain Escape

Valsassina is the ideal refuge if you're looking for a tranquil mountain getaway from the beaches of Lake Como. This gorgeous valley is located in the Prealps of Lombardy and offers a calm environment surrounded by thick woods, alpine meadows, and breathtaking peaks. It is just a short drive from Lake Como. What you may discover and do in Valsassina is as follows:

Scenic drives: Driving over winding mountain roads with stunning views of the valley and surrounding mountains is a delight in and of itself on the way to Valsassina.

Outdoor Activities: Valsassina is a paradise for nature lovers. You may go through stunning landscapes like the Pian delle Betulle plateau or the imposing Grigne mountains on hiking paths of varied degrees of difficulty.

Pian delle Betulle: is a lovely mountain town without any cars that may be reached from Margno by cable car. It's a wonderful location to relax, appreciate nature, and take in breathtaking aerial views of Lake Como.

Winter Sports: During the winter, snow sport fans flock to Valsassina as a playground. Among other ski areas, Piani di Bobbio and Artavaggio also provides skiing and snowboarding chances.

Local Cuisine: Local trattorias and mountain cottages serve up authentic Lombard food. Enjoy substantial foods like polenta, pizzoccheri, and cheeses that are produced locally.

Abbadia Lariana: This charming lakeside hamlet is just a short drive from Valsassina, says Abbadia Lariana. Explore its quaint alleys and old church or visit its pebble beach and unwind by the lake.

Waterfalls and Nature: Discover the stunning Orrido di Bellano canyon and the flowing waterfalls of Troggia, both of which provide chances for relaxing hikes through nature.

Relaxation and wellness: The area's many wellness facilities and spas provide opportunities to relax and revitalise among the tranquil mountain surroundings.

Traditional Festivals: Depending on when you visit, you can come across local celebrations and events that highlight the customs, music, and folk dances of the area.

Products made locally: Valsassina is renowned for its handicraft, which includes woodworking and the creation of the traditional wooden clogs known as "ciaspole." Bring some genuine mementos home.

The natural splendour and serenity of this area will capture your attention whether you go to Valsassina for an adventurous mountain getaway or a serene retreat. During your time in Lake Tahoe, embrace a slower pace of life, connect with nature, and experience the allure of this mountain retreat.

Lake Piano: Peace Among the Natural World

On the northernmost point of Lake Como sits a hidden treasure called Lake Piano, sometimes known as Lago di Piano. In comparison to its well-known neighbour, Lake Como, it is a smaller and less popular lake. For those looking for a relaxing break, Lake Piano provides a serene and tranquil ambiance among nature. What makes Lake Piano a special place to visit is as follows:

Pristine Setting: The pristine surroundings and crystal-clear waters of Lake Piano are its defining features. A tranquil and attractive scene is created by the marshes, reed beds, and lush vegetation that surround the lake.

Bird Watching Paradise: A paradise for birdwatchers, the lake's marshlands and reed beds are home to a variety of bird species. Watch out for the area's many lovely birds, including herons, kingfishers, and more.

Nature Walks: There are a number of walking routes around Lake Piano, allowing tourists to discover the area's stunning natural surroundings. Take a leisurely walk at the lake's edge or go on longer treks in the neighbouring Pian di Spagna Nature Reserve.

Peaceful Atmosphere: Because Lake Piano is less well-known and has a peaceful atmosphere, it is seldom busy, giving tourists an opportunity to appreciate the isolation and peace of nature.

Fishing: Anglers will value Lake Piano's tranquillity, where they may test their luck and unwind on a sunny day by the lake.

Drives with Beautiful Views: The trip from Lake Como to Lake Piano offers beautiful views of the surrounding mountains and the breathtaking natural surroundings.

Opportunities for Photography: Lake Piano's pristine beauty makes for a wonderful picture background. Take pictures of the fauna and the reflections on the tranquil waters.

Nature Retreat: Lake Piano provides a serene natural getaway for individuals who enjoy the outdoors and want to get away from the rush and bustle of everyday life.

Although Lake Piano may not be as well-known as Lake Como, its beauty rests in its simplicity and the chance to lose oneself in the peace of nature. Lake Piano is a tranquil retreat that offers a feeling of quiet and harmony among the natural beauties of the area, whether you come for a leisurely walk, birding, or just to rest and enjoy the peaceful ambiance.

Villa Monastero Varenna

On the eastern bank of Lake Como in Italy, near the quaint hamlet of Varenna, sits the magnificent ancient home known as Villa Monastero. This amazing mansion has a long and illustrious past that dates back to the 12th century, when it was first built as a Cistercian abbey. It underwent several modifications and additions throughout the years, culminating in the stunning architectural treasure we see today. Here are some reasons to visit Villa Monastero in Varenna:

Architecture and history: Due to the villa's beginnings as a Cistercian abbey, its past is rich in religious importance. It transformed into a beautiful aristocratic home throughout the years, with each era putting its stamp on the villa's architecture and interior design.

Beautiful Gardens: The large and lovely botanical gardens of Villa Monastero are one of the property's principal attractions. These

149.

well-kept gardens, which stretch for almost two kilometres along the lakefront, have a varied assortment of plants, flowers, and old trees. The Terrace Garden, Moorish Garden, Cypress Avenue, and Long Garden are just a few of the themed gardens that guests may explore.

Lakeside Location: Villa Monastero is located on the banks of Lake Como, in a prime lakeside location. The villa's charm is enhanced by the stunning views of the lake and the neighbouring mountains, which make it the perfect location for leisurely strolls and picturesque photography.

Science and Culture: The "House of Science," a global hub for scientific research and cultural interaction, is located at Villa Monastero, giving it a scientific and cultural component. The villa serves as a centre for scholarly activities because of the centre's hosting of conferences, seminars, and cultural events.

Museum and Exhibition: The Museum of the Lariosaurus, a showcase for local fossils, is located within the villa and is open to guests.

The estate also holds sporadic cultural events and exhibits of art.

Venue for weddings: Villa Monastero is a popular choice for weddings and other special occasions because of its beautiful environment. Beautiful festivities may be held against the exquisite background of the ancient buildings and gorgeous grounds.

Guided Tours:estate Monastero provides guided tours that shed light on the history, architectural intricacies, and floral riches of the estate. Visitors are accompanied by knowledgeable experts around the rooms, gardens, and displays, providing a fuller appreciation of this special location.

On Lake Como, Villa Monastero is a real treasure, combining natural beauty, history, and culture to offer a memorable experience. Villa Monastero in Varenna is a location that charms tourists with its beauty and elegance, whether they are interested in history, architecture, botanical gardens, or just seeking a calm lakeside hideaway.

Orrido di Bellano: The Bellano George

The Bellano Gorge, often referred to as the Orrido di Bellano, is a stunning natural marvel that can be seen near the Italian town of Bellano on the eastern bank of Lake Como. The Pioverna River's waters cut a tight valley over thousands of years, creating this stunning geological feature. When you visit the Orrido di Bellano, you'll have an exciting experience as you travel along walkways hanging over the gorge and get to see nature's unbridled force up close. What makes the Orrido di Bellano an exceptional and intriguing attraction is as follows:

Striking Natural Beauty: The Bellano Gorge is proof of the powerful erosional power of water. Over time, the Pioverna River cut a valley that is deep and narrow, with towering cliffs rising on each side, through the rock formations.

Suspended Walkway: Visitors may explore the Orrido di Bellano by walking over a number of platforms and hanging walkways that are attached to the gorge's rocky walls. These pathways provide a fascinating and secure approach to explore the gorge's interior.

Rapids & Waterfalls: The Orrido di Bellano is home to breathtaking waterfalls, as well as the raging noises of the river's rapids. The experience is engrossing and intense because of the rushing waves.

Natural pools: The river's erosive force has carved out a number of natural ponds throughout the valley. The deep, clear waters of these pools contribute to the lovely surroundings.

Lighting: The Orrido di Bellano is lit at night, which gives the canyon a magnificent atmosphere as the lights reflect off the rocks and the rushing water, changing it into a hypnotic show.

Historical Significance: The Orrido di Bellano is also of historical importance. The gorge formerly supplied energy to nearby sawmills and mills. Along the walk, you may still observe the ruins of these old buildings.

Guided Tours & Information: The Orrido di Bellano provides educational exhibits and guided tours that shed light on the development of the canyon, its geological characteristics, and the local flora and wildlife.

Family-friendly Experiences: The Orrido di Bellano is a kid- and family-friendly attraction because of the hanging walkways and safety precautions.

You may connect with the powers of nature and be in awe of this natural wonder by visiting the Orrido di Bellano, which is an exhilarating and instructive experience. This voyage into the Bellano Gorge's interior is unforgettably beautiful due to the harmony of the surrounding natural features, the suspended walkways, and the sounds of the flowing stream

Piona Abbey: A Place for Meditation

Piona Abbey, also known as Abbazia di Piona, is a beautiful and historic Cistercian abbey situated close to the Italian town of Colico on the eastern coast of Lake Como. This ancient place of worship provides a serene and spiritual haven where guests may lose themselves in the serene atmosphere of the abbey and its environs. What makes Piona Abbey a unique location for a spiritual retreat is as follows:

Rich History and Architecture: Piona Abbey was established by Cistercian monks in the 12th century and has a rich architectural history. The tranquil cloister of the abbey is a centrepiece of the complex, and the building's design displays Romanesque and Gothic elements.

Peaceful Location: Piona Abbey is located in a tranquil and attractive setting on a promontory with a view of Lake Como. An environment of peace and introspection is produced by the breathtaking lake vistas and the surrounding natural splendour.

Spiritual Traditions: For many years, Piona Abbey has served as a centre of prayer, meditation, and introspection. Visitors are welcome to join in liturgical services and experience the abbey's spirituality.

Guided Tours and Exhibitions: You may take a guided tour of the abbey's interior to see the cathedral, cloister, and monks' quarters. Additionally, the abbey presents exhibits that provide light on its historical and spiritual importance.

Herbal Medicine and Products: The monks of Piona Abbey, which is renowned for its herbal medical heritage, create herbal cures and cosmetics following traditional methods. These goods are available for sale to tourists as gifts or for personal use.

Botanical Garden: There is a tranquil botanical garden at the abbey with a huge variety of herbs and medicinal plants. The garden offers an opportunity to commune with nature and experience its therapeutic qualities.

Silence and Solitude: Piona Abbey provides the possibility for calm and alone, giving it the perfect setting for introspective activities including personal contemplation, meditation, and introspection.

Cultural Events and Concerts: Piona Abbey offers cultural events, concerts, and sacred music performances all year long that enhance the experience of visitors and contribute to the spiritual environment.

Natural Hiking and Walking Routes: The abbey is surrounded by natural hiking and walking paths, offering peaceful strolls and exploration of the lakeshore and the surrounding hills.

For individuals looking for spiritual refreshment and a connection to history and environment, Piona Abbey provides a tranquil and reflective retreat. Piona Abbey offers a deep experience in the centre of Lake Como's splendour, whether you are interested in religious traditions, architectural wonders, or just desire a tranquil refuge.

ENGAGING IN LOCAL FESTIVALS AND EVENTS

Como City of Toys (Como Città dei Balocchi)

The lovely and joyous festival known as Como Città dei Balocchi, or "Como City of Toys," takes place during the Christmas season in the Italian city of Como. The city is transformed into a winter paradise with entrancing decorations, lights, and a plethora of events that bring the Christmas spirit to life. What to anticipate from the Como Città dei Balocchi festival is as follows:

Christmas Lights & Decorations: With sparkling Christmas lights and festive accents covering the streets, squares, and buildings, Como comes to life. The city is completely lit up, providing a magnificent ambiance for both locals and tourists.

Christmas Market: The Christmas market, one of Como Città dei Balocchi's biggest attractions, has a variety of booths offering traditional Christmas decorations, crafts, presents, and regional specialties.

Ice Skating: During the celebrations, Como puts up an ice skating rink, offering people of all ages a great pastime to enjoy skating on the ice against the background of lovely Christmas lights.

Santa Claus and other Christmas figures: are available for children to meet throughout the celebration, ensuring that it is a happy and enjoyable experience for them.

Nativity Scenes: Como is well-known for its beautiful nativity scenes, and during Città dei Balocchi, the city puts up elaborate and imaginative nativity scenes in a number of sites, exhibiting Italian craftsmanship and the Christmas spirit.

Christmas Concerts and plays: To heighten the holiday atmosphere, the city holds Christmas concerts, carol singing and live plays. Visitors are entertained by the uplifting versions of traditional Christmas songs performed by local choirs and musicians.

Workshops & Activities: Opportunities to make Christmas crafts and decorations are provided during workshops for kids and families. It's a wonderful opportunity for families to connect and celebrate the season.

Puppet Shows & Entertainment: As part of the celebration's entertainment schedule, puppet shows and street performances will make the spectators smile and laugh.

Culinary Delights: Como's eateries and cafés celebrate the holiday season by dishing up traditional Christmas fare and merry delights, letting customers enjoy the tastes of the time of year.

The lovely and endearing Como Città dei Balocchi festival invites locals and tourists together to enjoy the wonder of Christmas. It's a wonderful time to visit Como during the Christmas season because of the city's joyful atmosphere, events, and activities, which make for a memorable experience for everyone.

St. John's Festival, or Sagra di San Giovanni

The St. John's Festival, also known as Sagra di San Giovanni, is an annual festival celebrated in a number of Italian towns and cities, including Como and the villages around Lake Como. The celebration is held on June 24, which is St. John the Baptist's Day, an important holiday in Christianity. The Sagra di San Giovanni is a colourful and happy occasion that mixes religious customs with social celebrations. What to anticipate from the Como St. John's Festival is as follows:

Religious Procession: A religious procession through Como's streets traditionally ushers in the festivities. Members of the clergy and followers carry a statue or relic of St. John the Baptist while singing songs and praying.

Fireworks: The stunning fireworks show that lights up the night sky over Lake Como is one of the Sagra di San Giovanni's primary attractions. The fireworks are often launched from boats on the lake, producing an amazing display.

Boat parade: Since Como is a city on Lake Como, the event often features a boat procession. On the lake, boats adorned with lights and flags float, enhancing the joyful mood.

Bonfires and torchlight processions: are part of the festivities in certain cities, signifying the cleansing and rebirth that are linked with the feast of St. John the Baptist.

Traditional Food and Drinks: During the Sagra di San Giovanni, regional delicacies and traditional Italian cuisine are served at food stalls and neighbourhood eateries. As part of the celebrations, visitors may savour a range of delectable foods and beverages.

Music and Dancing: traditional dances, and other forms of entertainment are all part of the event, which keeps the people amused and upbeat.

Religious mass and Blessings: Along with the processions, fireworks, and celebrations, a religious service is celebrated in remembrance of St. John the Baptist. The gathering audience may get blessings from the priest as well.

Cultural Activities: The St. John's Festival offers a chance to get a taste of the customs, traditions, and culture of the Italian community. Visitors may see the vibrant feeling of community and the folk customs of Italy.

The Sagra di San Giovanni is a well-known event that brings the neighbourhood together to remember St. John the Baptist's feast day and welcome summer. The St. John's Festival provides a genuine and unforgettable experience of Italian culture and customs in the lovely backdrop of Lake Como, whether you're taking part in the religious services, watching the fireworks, or just taking in the joyful mood.

Festival of san Nicolò in Lecco

Italy's scenic town of Lecco, which is situated on the southeast beaches of Lake Como, hosts the annual Festival of San Nicol. The patron saint of sailors and fishermen, Saint Nicholas, also known as San Nicol in Italian, is honoured during the festival. On December 6, which is Saint Nicholas's Day, the festivity is held. In Lecco, the Festival of San Nicol is a time for celebration, socialising, and cultural events. What to anticipate from this joyous event is as follows:

Religious Procession: The festival starts out with a religious procession in which parishioners and clergy carry a statue or relic of Saint Nicholas through the streets of Lecco. Hymns and prayers are played as the procession moves.

Blessing of the Boats: Lecco commemorates its ties to Saint Nicholas, the patron saint of sailors, as a town with a rich nautical history. On the shores of Lake Como during the event, boats and other vessels are often adorned and paraded. The boats and their crew get a special blessing for safety and secure trips.

Fireworks Show: A magnificent fireworks show over Lake Como heralds the Festival of San Nicol. The vibrant fireworks illuminate the night sky, providing the gathering audience with a breathtaking visual treat.

Cultural and artistic activities: are often presented during the festival, including musical concerts, traditional dances, and theatre productions. These events highlight the local community's talented individuals and rich history.

Local cuisine: is available at food stands and merchants throughout the event, along with a selection of typical Italian fare. Delicious food and beverages are available for visitors to enjoy while taking in the festive ambiance.

Activities for Children: The Festival of San Nicol is a family-friendly festival, and a number of events are planned for kids, including games, shows, and appearances by Santa Claus, who resembles Saint Nicholas.

Street Markets: During the festival, street markets are set up where residents and guests may explore and buy handicrafts, mementos, and holiday presents.

Religious Mass and Blessings: To commemorate Saint Nicholas, a religious service is celebrated, and those in attendance may receive blessings.

Lecco's Festival of San Nicol is a beloved occasion that brings the neighbourhood together to recognize their nautical history, honour their patron saint, and take in the joyous holiday atmosphere. This festival is a wonderful and cherished memory for both residents and tourists since it combines religious traditions, cultural events, and happy gatherings.

SUSTAINABLE TRAVEL AND RESPONSIBLE TOURISM

Como Film Festival

In the beautiful Italian city of Como, there is an annual celebration of film art known as the

Como Film Festival. This film festival presents a broad range of domestic and foreign films, including feature-length films, short films, documentaries, and cartoons. The festival's objectives include fostering fresh talent, promoting cinema culture, and giving filmmakers a venue to exhibit their work. What to anticipate from the Como Film Festival is as follows:

Movie showings: The Como Film Festival's main event is the showing of a broad range of movies with various subjects and genres. The films available to audiences include both popular and indie productions as well as works by up-and-coming directors.

International Participation: The Como Film Festival brings together filmmakers, producers, and movie buffs from all over the globe, promoting intercultural dialogue and celebrating the unifying power of cinema.

Competitions & Awards: The festival often holds film contests where a number of accolades are up for grabs, such as Best Film, Best Director, Best Actor/Actress, and more.

These prizes honour outstanding achievements to the film industry.

Q&A Sessions and Workshops: Film makers and industry experts regularly take part in Q&A sessions and seminars, offering insightful commentary on the filmmaking process and igniting debates regarding the films shown.

Special Screenings: In addition to the official choices, the Como Film Festival may hold unique showings of vintage movies, cult classics, and retrospective showcases in honour of the evolution of cinema.

Gala evenings & Red Carpet Events: The festival offers opulent gala evenings and red carpet events to add a little sparkle and intrigue to the celebration of movies.

Networking in the film business: The Como Film Festival provides a venue for filmmakers, producers, and industry experts to connect, work together, and consider prospective projects.

Film Location Tours: Como's gorgeous surroundings and history as a shooting site for several movies draw movie buffs to the city to explore areas used in movies.

The Como Film Festival is a cultural festival that brings together film lovers, artists, and filmmakers to celebrate the wonder of creating a narrative through the medium of film. It is not only a chance to see excellent movies. Both experts in the film business and movie buffs will find the festival to be a remarkable and enlightening experience due to its lively environment and emphasis on creative expression.

Como Music Festival

The enchanting Italian city of Como hosts the Como Music Festival every year. This festival honours music by bringing together accomplished musicians, well-known artists, and music lovers from a variety of genres and backgrounds. The Como Music Festival strives to highlight the area's rich musical tradition, provide up-and-coming performers a stage, and present its audience with unique performances. What to anticipate from the Como Music Festival is as follows:

Various Musical Performances:A wide variety of musical genres, including classical, jazz, opera, contemporary, folk, and world music, are performed throughout the festival. In distinctive and beautiful venues all across Como, audiences may take in a range of musical genres and styles.

Renowned Musicians: International and domestically renowned artists perform in the Como Music Festival, showcasing their extraordinary skills. Renowned orchestras, groups, and singers often play during the event.

Outdoor Concerts: A few concerts are held in Como's picturesque outdoor sites, such lakeside venues or significant squares, enabling audiences to enjoy music among the city's breathtaking surroundings.

Indoor Concerts in Historic Locations: Other concerts take place inside historical locations like theatres, cathedrals, and cultural organisations, which give the music a compelling atmosphere.

Special Collaboration: Premieres of new works and exceptional collaborations between artists are frequent events during the Como Music Festival, which provide distinctive and unforgettable musical experiences.

Music Workshop: Workshops and masterclasses in music may be offered as part of the festival, giving students and aspiring musicians the chance to study from accomplished performers and instructors.

Events that are accessible and welcoming to families: The Como Music Festival features performances and events that are appropriate for audiences of all ages.

Cultural Exchange: The event promotes music as a global language that unites individuals from various origins by inviting performers from across the globe.

Pre- and post-concert activities: may enhance the musical experience by providing opportunity for pre-concert lectures, post-concert meet-and-greets, and other opportunities to connect with the musicians.

The Como Music Festival is a vibrant festival of music that values creative quality, variety, and a common love of the genre. It provides a chance to immerse oneself in the music world and be mesmerised by the exceptional musical abilities of outstanding performers against the entrancing background of Como's cultural history.

Lake Como Environmental Initiatives

The sustainability and protection of the environment are issues that Lake Como and many other pristine natural regions are becoming more and more concerned about. Numerous programs have been put in place to safeguard the habitat and surrounds of the lake. These programs attempt to solve problems including pollution, climate change, the preservation of wildlife, and sustainable tourism. Around Lake Como, important environmental activities include:

Water Quality Management: Through the installation of wastewater treatment facilities, efficient waste disposal, and actions to stop contamination from industrial and agricultural operations, efforts have been made to monitor and enhance the water quality of Lake Como.

Biodiversity Conservation: By creating protected areas and natural reserves, Lake Como's distinctive biodiversity is being safeguarded. These locations act as wildlife sanctuaries and contribute to the preservation of different plant and animal species' natural habitats.

Reforestation and Green Spaces: Reforestation and the development of green spaces are initiatives that seek to improve the natural environment, the quality of the air, and the availability of recreational places for both inhabitants and visitors.

Sustainable Tourism Practices: Local governments and companies are supporting sustainable tourism practices to lessen the damaging effects of tourism on the environment. Promoting eco-friendly lodging, encouraging responsible travel, and providing eco-tours that educate guests about the lake's natural history are just a few of the initiatives being made.

Climate Change Adaptation: The sensitive ecology of Lake Como faces difficulties from climate change. Initiatives that manage water resources, protect vulnerable ecosystems, and put in place energy-saving measures all aim to adapt to changing circumstances.

Waste Reduction and Recycling: Waste management programs have been implemented to lessen plastic pollution and promote recycling, while public awareness campaigns try to inform locals and tourists of the value of properly reducing trash and recycling.

Sustainable Fishing Practices: Fish populations should be protected, and sustainable fishing methods should be used to preserve a healthy aquatic environment. Regulations and standards protect the viability of the lake's fisheries by preventing overfishing.

Environmental Education and Awareness: To spread knowledge about environmental challenges and the value of conserving Lake Como's natural beauty for future generations, educational programs and campaigns are run

By combining these environmental programs, local governments, organisations, and communities show their dedication to protecting Lake Como's natural resources and ensuring their long-term viability. These initiatives are essential to maintaining the appeal and ecological integrity of one of Italy's most famous and treasured locations.

Eco-friendly Tours and Activities

Numerous environmentally friendly excursions and activities are available in Lake Como, allowing guests to take in the area's splendour while having as little of an effect as possible. These initiatives support environmentally friendly behaviours and a love of the outdoors. You may engage in the following eco-friendly pursuits in Lake Como:

Electric Boat Tour: Choose electric boat trips to discover Lake Como's breathtaking sceneries rather than typical motorboat tours. Electric boats are an environmentally responsible way to take in the beauty of the lake since they are quieter and emit no pollutants.

Cycling and hiking: Take a hike or a bike ride around Lake Como's picturesque footpaths and roads. There are several hiking and bike trails that minimise your carbon impact while providing spectacular views of the lake and the mountains in the area.

Kayaking and Stand-Up Paddleboarding (SUP): Get a close-up view of Lake Como's serenity by kayaking or SUP. You may take pleasure in the peace of the lake while being kind to the environment by participating in these non-motorized water sports.

Bird Watching & Nature Walks: Take part in a guided birding tour or a nature walk to explore the local flora and animals. Discover the biodiversity of the area and the conservation efforts being made while observing the natural environments.

Sustainable Cooking lessons: Enrol in lessons that emphasise utilising organic, locally produced foods and conventional culinary techniques. Discover the history of the area's cuisine and its commitment to sustainable agriculture.

Organic farms Visit: Lake Como is a great way to learn about sustainable agricultural methods and show your support for them.

Solar powered Ferries: Take the ferries that are powered by solar energy to go between the many communities on the lake. These boats run on clean energy and provide a beautiful, tranquil form of transportation.

Volunteering and cleanup Activities: Participate in neighbourhood-led volunteer projects or cleanup efforts around Lake Como to help keep the area's natural beauty intact.

Eco-Friendly Accommodations: Opt for eco-friendly hotels, inns, or bed and breakfasts that place a high value on environmental preservation and sustainable business operations.

Responsible Wildlife Tours: If you're interested in wildlife encounters, choose an itinerary that puts animals' welfare and the preservation of their habitats first.

You may fully enjoy Lake Como's natural splendours while promoting ethical and sustainable tourism by taking part in these eco-friendly excursions. By participating in these activities, you may connect with the area's beauty while also doing your part to protect it for future generations to enjoy.

Supporting Local Communities and Businesses

A significant method to benefit Lake Como and its surroundings is to support neighbourhood organisations and businesses. Here are some ideas on how you may support the local economy and preserve the region's distinctive traditions and culture:

Buy products and keepsakes from neighbourhood businesses, marketplaces, and artisanal shops. Purchasing goods created locally not only benefits the community's economy but also aids in the preservation of traditional crafts and skills.

Dine at Local Restaurants: Choose to dine at restaurants and eateries that are owned and operated locally, provide regional cuisine, and obtain their ingredients locally. Local cuisine maintains the region's culinary traditions and directly improves the neighbourhood's economy.

Choose local Accommodation: Stay at hotels, guesthouses, or bed & breakfasts that are locally owned. Supporting neighbourhood lodging helps to maintain the lives of service industry employees and enhances the general economic health of the neighbourhood.

Participate in Local Events: Attend local festivals, musical performances, and cultural events to learn about the distinctive traditions and practices of the area. Your participation fosters community involvement and aids in the preservation of cultural heritage.

Use Local Services: Take advantage of locally owned and operated businesses that provide services like excursions, transportation, and guided tours. You support the livelihoods of regional tour operators and businesses by doing this.

Support sustainable practices Always: Select travel agencies and companies that emphasise sustainable and green operations. Supporting efforts that are ecologically friendly helps in preserving Lake Como's natural beauty for future generations.

Participate in the Community Life: Maintain a polite and cordial relationship with the locals. Interacting with locals may promote mutual understanding and beneficial cultural interactions.

Consider volunteering for neighbourhood: projects or programs that advance social welfare, education, or environmental preservation. Making a contribution of your time and abilities may benefit the neighbourhood.

Respect the environment and regional customs: Respect the nature, traditions, and customs of the area. In order to practise responsible tourism, one must leave as little of an environmental and cultural impact as possible.

Leave Positive Reviews: If you've had a good experience with a local company or service, post a nice review online or tell others about it. Local companies may develop greatly with the support of word-of-mouth referrals.

You may help to ensure the long-term sustainability of the area while also maintaining Lake Como's special beauty and personality by giving your support to neighbourhood organisations and businesses. Your decisions as a responsible tourist may have an impact on preserving the authenticity and means of subsistence of locals who call this beautiful location home.

TRAVELLING WITH KIDS AND FAMILY FRIENDLY PLACES

Family-friendly Places to Visit

Visitors of all ages may enjoy a wide range of family-friendly sights and activities in Lake Como. The area has plenty to offer for everyone, whether you're travelling with small children or teens. The following are some family-friendly places to visit around Lake Como:

Lido di Bellagio is a well-liked, kid-friendly beach where you can unwind by the lake, swim, and take in the sunshine. The beach is furnished with amenities including sun loungers, umbrellas, and kids' play areas.

Jungle Raider Park: A family-friendly adventure park with tree-top trails, zip lines, and obstacle courses is located close to Civenna. It's a wonderful way to enjoy the area's natural beauty while learning about it.

Villa Carlotta: In Tremezzina, Villa Carlotta is a lovely property with lovely grounds that is ideal for a leisurely walk with the family. Children will delight in navigating the walkways and finding secret nooks as they explore the gardens, which are home to a large variety of plants and flowers.

Menaggio Lido: A swimming pool, water slides, and playgrounds can be found at this family-friendly beach. It's a great place to spend the day by the lake and engage in different water sports.

Como-Brunate Funicular : Enjoy the lovely trip to Brunate while taking in the panoramic views of the lake and the surrounding mountains. Explore Brunate after you arrive, go on short treks, and have lunch while taking in the scenery.

Villa Melzi Gardens: Families may stroll peacefully and picturesquely in Bellagio's Villa Melzi Gardens while taking in the quiet splendour of Lake Como.

AcquaWorld Concorezzo: is an indoor water park with slides, pools, and water activities that will occupy kids of all ages. It is situated close to Lake Como.

Cadenabbia Mini Golf: A good family activity is mini golf in Cadenabbia. Mini-golf matches are held amongst rivals in a lovely lakeside environment.

Educational Boat Tours: Take a boat excursion around Lake Como. Many companies provide family-friendly boat cruises with kid-friendly, educational guides.

Como-Brunate Cycling Path: The Como-Brunate cycling path is a kid- and family-friendly route that provides a leisurely and picturesque ride around the lake.

These family-friendly destinations provide a variety of outdoor activities, cultural encounters, and enjoyable pastimes for both children and adults. Lake Como is a wonderful family holiday location, whether you want to play by the lake, explore gardens, or go on an adventure.

Child-Friendly Cafes & Restaurants

There are several eateries and cafés in Lake Como that welcome families with small children. These places make eating with kids enjoyable by providing a friendly ambiance, kid-friendly menus, and amenities. Here are several eateries and cafés around Lake Como that welcome kids:

Varenna Esino Beach: is a lakeside restaurant with a large outdoor patio and lovely views of the lake. It is situated in Varenna. Pizza, spaghetti, and other kid-friendly dishes are available on the menu.

La Fabbrica del Gelato: is a favourite of both children and adults. While exploring Bellagio's lovely streets, savour a broad range of tantalising gelato varieties

Ristorante Pizzeria Bilacus: The family-friendly Bellagio eatery Ristorante Pizzeria Bilacus offers top-notch pizzas and pasta dishes. Families with kids will love the outside dining area.

Pizzeria Balognett: Situated in Menaggio, this pizzeria provides a comfortable and relaxed atmosphere. Kids' pizza alternatives are available on the vast pizza menu, and the staff is attentive to families.

Bar Gelateria Lariana: enjoy the gelato, pastries, and snacks at Como's Gelateria Lariana. It's the ideal place to stop and rest while exploring the heart of Como.

II Crott del Meo :is a Como restaurant with a kid's menu and a friendly ambiance. The family will enjoy the classic Italian foods that are served there.

Ristorante Pizzeria La Baia: is a family-friendly eatery located in Menaggio with a varied menu that includes pizzas, pastas, and seafood dishes. For families, the outside sitting area offers a tranquil backdrop.

Gelateria Lariana: This Como gelateria is renowned for its premium gelato and a variety of flavours that youngsters will love.

The Bellagio restaurant Osteria: la Tana dei Pescatori has a cosy and welcoming atmosphere. Children may eat the pasta selections and fish entrees.

Trattoria del Porto: has a kid-friendly cuisine and a welcoming atmosphere for families. It's a great option for a casual family lunch.

The restaurants and cafés around Lake Como that welcome kids make eating with kids a joyful experience. Families may enjoy delectable meals together while visiting Lake Como since they provide a variety of Italian specialties, kid-friendly alternatives, and a warm atmosphere.

Outdoor Activities for Kids

Kids may engage in a variety of outdoor activities around Lake Como and the surrounding surroundings. Children may engage with nature, have fun, and create enduring memories while participating in these activities. Here are several kid-friendly outdoor pursuits around Lake Como:

Boat Rides on Lake Como: Take a boat trip on Lake Como to take in the breathtaking views and the feeling of being on the water. The thrill of being on a boat and taking in the gorgeous lakeside villages will be enjoyed much by children.

Nature Walks & Hikes: Take a stroll along one of the numerous walking paths or hike with your family around Lake Como. Kids of all ages and fitness levels may enjoy the area's picturesque trails.

Wildlife Watching: Be on the lookout for animals around Lake Como. Kids will enjoy seeing the many species that live around the lake, including the ducks, birds, and other creatures.

playground Fun: There are playgrounds in a lot of the villages around Lake Como where kids may climb, swing, and play with other kids.

Swimming and Water Activities: Children may enjoy swimming in the lake or playing in the shallow waters next to the beaches during the warmer months.

Bike Rides: Ride a bike with the family along the lakeshore or into the picturesque countryside by renting bicycles. In many locations, there are kid-friendly bike trails.

Mini Golf: Play a round of friendly mini golf with the family at a location close to Lake Como.

Adventure Parks: For an adrenaline-fueled day of excitement, older children can visit adventure parks featuring zip lines, treetop trails, and obstacle courses.

Botanical Gardens: Take the kids to the lovely botanical gardens around Lake Como, such as the grounds at Villa Carlotta, where they can explore the lush foliage and discover different plant species.

Rock Skimming: Children may practise their rock-skimming techniques in Lake Como's calm waters.

Horseback Riding: Take a kid-friendly guided horseback riding excursion to see the countryside.

Children may enjoy the natural beauty and leisure pleasures that Lake Como has to offer via these outdoor activities. Lake Como is a wonderful playground for kids and families to enjoy together, whether it's boating, hiking, or just taking in the great outdoors.

PRACTICAL TIPS FOR LAKE COMO TRAVEL

Safety and Emergency Information.

Anywhere you go, even Lake Como, you need to be safe. Following are some safety advice and emergency contact details to have in mind when travelling:

Tips for general safety

Keep an eye on your possessions and try to keep expensive items hidden.

a. Be mindful of your surroundings, particularly in busy tourist locations.

b.Passports and travel insurance papers should be kept in a safe location.

c.Keep yourself hydrated, particularly in hot weather, and apply sunscreen to avoid being burned.

Water Safety Tips:

a.If you want to swim in Lake Como, be mindful of the depth, currents, and water quality.

b.Pay heed to any caution warnings and only swim in specified locations.

c.Children should always be properly watched while near water.

Road Safety:

a.Follow all traffic laws and regulations while driving. Drive on the right side of the road in Italy.

b.Make sure child seats are fitted correctly for small children and always use seat belts.

c.Consider taking public transit or hiring a local driver if you are unfamiliar with the driving conditions in your destination area.

Emergency Contact Information: Dial these numbers in case of an emergency:

a.Emergency Medical Services: 118 (ambulance)

b.Police 112

c.Fire Department 115

Healthcare: Learn where the closest hospitals and medical facilities are located. There are hospitals and pharmacies in a few significant towns around Lake Como.

Travel Insurance: Make sure you have comprehensive travel insurance that covers medical emergencies, trip cancellations, and other unexpected incidents before you go on your vacation.

Weather: During your visit, be cautious of the weather conditions. Be ready for dramatic fluctuations in temperature and rainfall during particular seasons when the weather surrounding Lake Como might change quickly.

Language: Even though English is frequently spoken in tourist regions, it might be useful to acquire a few fundamental Italian words to make conversation easier, particularly in more isolated places.

Emergency Exit Strategy: Know how to evacuate in case of emergency at your lodging, and follow any instructions that are given.

Observe local regulations: During your tour, be aware of any applicable local laws or regulations, particularly those that touch on COVID-19 procedures.

You may thoroughly enjoy your time at Lake Como and have a memorable and trouble-free experience in this lovely place by putting safety first and remaining informed.

Local Customs and Etiquette

To show respect for the local culture and traditions, it is important to be aware of local etiquette and customs while visiting Lake Como and its surroundings. To remember, have the following in mind:

Greeting:handshake is the customary way to introduce yourself when meeting someone for the first time in Italy. Close friends and family members may kiss each other on both cheeks when they first meet. If you are addressing someone you don't know well, use formal titles (such as Signore for Mr. and Signora for Mrs.).

Dress Code: Italy often has a smart-casual dress code, particularly in metropolitan areas.

When attending churches, religious places, or expensive restaurants, dress smartly and refrain from donning too casual or exposing apparel.

MealTime Etiquette:

a.Italians put a high value on meals and enjoy it when tourists observe their dietary traditions. Remember that supper is normally served later in the evening, from 7:30 to 9:00 PM, and that lunch is typically served from around 12:30 to 2:00 PM.

b.It's usual to wait for everyone at the table to be served before beginning to eat while eating out.

c.Don't hurry through your lunch since Italians often linger.

Tipping: As a service fee is often included into the bill, tipping is less popular in Italy than in some other nations. But it's always nice to give a little more for really great service.

Use of English: Although English is often spoken in tourist destinations, making an effort to use simple Italian expressions like "hello" (ciao/buongiorno), "please" (per favore), and "thank you" (grazie) is always welcomed and demonstrates respect for the local tongue.

Queuing: When waiting in line, particularly in public spaces or when on public transit, Italians are often courteous. Always wait for your turn after joining the back of the queue.

Public Behaviour:

a.Use a neutral speech tone while in public places like restaurants, museums, and transit.

b.Stay away from public shows of love that go beyond what is appropriate in public places.

Religious Site: Visit churches and other religious buildings in modest clothing, and refrain from making loud sounds or utilising flash photography.

Respect for Historical Sites and the Environment: When visiting historical sites, abide by the norms and regulations established by the government to protect the region's history and natural beauty. The same rules on littering and leaving no trace apply to outdoor areas like parks and hiking trails.

You may immerse yourself more fully in Lake Como's cultural experience and show respect for the people and places you come across by adhering to certain regional customs and traditions.

Transportation Tips

You can explore the area and its attractions with ease thanks to easy and convenient transportation surrounding Lake Como. The following transportation advice can help you have a seamless and pleasurable trip:

Ferries and boats: The cities and villages around Lake Como are connected by a vast network of ferries and boats. A beautiful and pleasurable method to go from one place to another is via boat. To plan your excursions, check the boat timetables in advance.

Public Buses: Around Lake Como, public buses run often and are an affordable means of transportation. Buses link cities and villages, making it simple to travel throughout the area. Examine the bus routes and timetables in advance.

Trains: Major cities like Milan are easily accessible by rail from Lake Como. Como San Giovanni and Varenna-Esino are the area's two main railway stations. Trains provide an easy method to get to Lake Como from different regions of Italy.

Car rentals: If you'd want greater freedom in your travels, think about doing so. You may go at your own leisure while exploring distant places and off-the-beaten-path locations if you have a vehicle. However, bear in mind that some cities have restricted parking and small streets, so drive carefully.

Cable cars and funiculars: Some Lake Como municipalities, such Como and Brunate, have cable cars and funiculars that take passengers to higher heights where they may enjoy beautiful views of the lake and its surroundings.

Cycling & Walking: Since many of the villages around Lake Como are pedestrian-friendly, seeing the neighbourhood's sights on foot is a delightful option. Cycling is another well-liked alternative, and some places provide bike rentals.

Ticket and Passes: Consider acquiring a Lake Como Transportation Pass, which offers unrestricted travel on trains, buses, and boats within the selected zones. If you intend to use public transit often, these passes provide convenience and financial benefits.

Plan Ahead: Before your trip to Lake Como, research the available modes of transportation and their timetables. Plan your itineraries after being familiar with the many available types of transportation.

Peak Season Consideration: It's a good idea to purchase tickets in advance whenever you can since transportation may be more congested during the busiest travel season.

Be Punctual: If you have a set timetable or a reservation, be careful to get to transit hubs like railway stations or ferry ports on time.

You may make the most of your stay at Lake Como by getting between its attractive villages, stunning scenery, and must-see sites effectively by following these transportation suggestions.

Language and Communication

Italian is the main language used in the Lake Como area. Despite the fact that English is often spoken in tourist regions and that many people employed in the tourism sector, particularly in hotels, restaurants, and stores, are fluent in the language, it is always appreciated when tourists make an attempt to speak a few simple Italian phrases. To assist you go around Lake Como, here are some basic Italian words and communication advice

Basic Phrases:
- Hello: Ciao / Buongiorno
- Goodbye: Arrivederci
- Please: Per favore
- Thank you: Grazie
- Yes: Sì
- No: No
- Excuse me / Sorry: Scusa / Mi scusi (formal)
- I don't understand: Non capisco

Greetings: The customary way to greet someone when meeting them for the first time is with a handshake. Close friends and family members may kiss each other on both cheeks when they first meet.

Polite Address: When speaking to strangers or in formal contexts, use formal titles (e.g., Signore for Mr. and Signora for Mrs.).

Pointing and Gestures: If you're having problems communicating, you may be able to do it by pointing at objects or using simple motions.

English Assistance: Many people in popular tourist destinations are used to engaging with English-speaking tourists and may give you directions or suggest places to go.

Phrasebooks and language apps: To assist you with popular phrases and translations, download a language app or have a phrasebook with you at all times.

Be Patient and Friendly: When interacting, be kind and patient. Even if you don't speak Italian well, being pleasant and smiling can help you connect with the people.

learn Names of Local places: Learn the names of the cities and tourist attractions you want to visit. When asking for directions or describing your plan, it will be beneficial to know how to pronounce certain words.

Speak Slowly: If you're trying to speak Italian, speak slowly and clearly to help others understand you, particularly if you're not sure how to pronounce certain words.

Remember that communication is an essential component of any trip, and making an effort to speak a few simple Italian words will improve your interactions with locals and enhance your whole Lake Como experience. Even if there are language issues, the majority of people are kind and accommodating, and a smile and a good outlook can get through a lot of challenges.

USEFUL PHRASES IN LAKE COMO

Here are some useful phrases in Italian that can be handy during your visit to Lake Como:

Ciao / Salve - Hello / Hi (informal / formal)

Buongiorno - Good morning / Good day

Buonasera - Good evening

Arrivederci - Goodbye

Grazie - Thank you

Per favore - Please

Scusa / Mi scusi (formal) - Excuse me / Sorry

Sì - Yes

No - No

Parla inglese? - Do you speak English?

Mi chiamo [Your Name] - My name is [Your Name]

Non capisco - I don't understand

Posso avere il conto, per favore? - Can I have the bill, please?

Quanto costa? - How much does it cost?

Dov'è il bagno? - Where is the restroom?

Vorrei un caffè, per favore. - I would like a coffee, please.

Mi piace molto! - I like it very much!

Che bella vista! - What a beautiful view!

Posso scattare una foto? - Can I take a photo?

Mi sono perso(a) - I am lost

During your stay in Lake Como, these words and phrases will assist you in navigating social situations, being courteous, and establishing relationships with locals. Even if it's only a few simple words, Italians typically enjoy it when foreigners try to speak their language. Enjoy your journey and Lake Como's special beauty!

SAMPLE ITINERARY

A 7-day schedule for Lake Como enables you to take in the region's major attractions, quaint villages, and natural beauty while still making time for leisurely activities and relaxation. A proposed 7-day Lake Como itinerary is shown below:

Day 1: Entry into Como

Arrive in Como, then relax into your lodging.

Explore the ancient city centre while taking a leisurely walk along the promenade that borders the lake.

Discover the Duomo di Como, a magnificent example of Gothic architecture.

Enjoy your first Italian lunch while unwinding at a neighbourhood café.

Day 2: Villa Melzi Gardens and Bellagio

Ride a beautiful ferry to Bellagio, often referred to as the "Pearl of Lake Como."

Discover the quaint village, stroll around its cobblestone streets, and browse the gift shops.

Visit the Villa Melzi Gardens, a lovely garden with breathtaking views of the lake and unusual vegetation.

Dinner by the lake is enjoyable in Bellagio.

Day 3

Take a boat to the charming fishing hamlet of Varenna.

Visit the magnificent Villa Monastero and its lovely gardens while exploring Varenna's winding alleyways.

Indulge in some peace and quiet at a lakeside café.

Consider taking a hike to the adjacent Castle of Vezio for sweeping vistas if you have the time

Day 4

Explore the luxurious Villa Carlotta in Tremezzo while you're there, complete with its beautiful gardens and art collection.

Take a boat out to Lake Como's lone island, Isola Comacina, and investigate the archeological remains there.

At the well-liked lakeside beach Lido di Lenno, unwind in the afternoon.

Day 5

Brunate and the Como-Brunate Funicular.

Visit Brunate via the Como-Brunate funicular for breathtaking views of Lake Como.

Discover the quaint town of Brunate, stroll along beautiful pathways, and have a meal with a view.

In the afternoon, return to Como and think about taking a boat excursion to a neighbouring village or just relax in Como.

Day 6

Visit Bergamo or Milan for the day

Visit Bergamo for the day; it is a lovely hilltop town with a charming ancient town (Città Alta).

Alternately, spend the day travelling to Milan to experience its historical sites, museums, and commercial areas.

In the evening, return to Como and take part in a goodbye meal.

Day 7

Departure

You could have some spare time, depending on the time of your departure, to finish up any last-minute souvenir buying or to spend a leisurely morning by the lake.

Bid Lake Como adieu and go off on your next adventure.

Please note that this schedule is just a recommendation; you may alter it to suit your needs and tastes. Adjust the plan to fit your speed and interests as Lake Como has a variety of sights and activities. Enjoy yourself and make enduring memories while you're in Lake Como!

Cooking courses in agriturismos (farmhouses): A few agriturismos around Lake Como provide cooking lessons that emphasise farm-to-table dishes using organic products and vegetables from their own farms.

Hotel cooking lessons: Some hotels and resorts, especially those that place a strong emphasis on cuisine, provide culinary lessons for its visitors. Ask your lodging whether they provide such experiences.

THE USE OF TELEPHONES AND TIPS

When visiting Lake Como, it's crucial to be aware of local customs about tipping and phone use. What you need to know is as follows:

Tipping: In contrast to some other nations, tipping is not as usual or anticipated in Italy. At restaurants, coffee shops, and hotels, particularly in popular locations like Lake Como, a service charge is often added to the bill.It is common to leave a little tip of between 5% and 10% for great service when there is no service fee included, although it is not required.

Taxi drivers are not expected to accept tips, however it is appreciated if you round up the fare to the closest Euro.Locals often leave a small amount of change as a tip at pubs and cafés, although it's not necessary.

Communication: Mobile network coverage is typically strong in Lake Como, so you shouldn't have any issues connecting while you're there.

If you're coming from overseas, ask your cell provider about their plans and prices for international roaming. If you want inexpensive data and telephony services, purchasing a local SIM card is an additional choice. Around Lake Como, there are several hotels, eateries, and cafés with free WiFi. Although they may not always be secure, use care when connecting to public Wi-Fi networks.

Communication via Language:

Italian is the major language spoken at Lake Como and across Italy. Even though English is frequently spoken in tourist regions, it's always welcomed when guests try to speak a little bit of Italian.

Knowing how to greet people, express gratitude, and ask for help in basic Italian words can improve your contacts with locals and demonstrate respect for their culture.

You may plan your vacation efficiently and guarantee nice encounters with locals during your stay by being aware of the tipping traditions and communications alternatives in Lake Como. Make the most of your stay in this stunning area by taking in all you can.

Guidelines for Packing list: Depending on when you want to travel and the activities you have in mind, you should prepare differently for Lake Como. This basic packing list will assist you in getting ready for your trip:

a.Summer apparel should be lightweight and breathable (June through August). Think about packing t-shirts, sundresses, shorts, and light tops.

b.Sandals or comfortable walking shoes for touring towns and enjoying leisurely strolls.

c.For chilly evenings—especially near the lake—bring along a light sweater or jacket.

d.If you're going in the spring or fall (April to May or September to October), bring a few layers and a lightweight jacket.

e.Swimwear is required since the waters of Lake Como are so clear. If you want to swim, don't forget to bring swimsuits, a beach towel, and water shoes.

f.Sun protection: Wear sunscreen with a high SPF to save your skin from harmful UV rays, particularly in the summer.

g.For sun protection, use sunglasses and a wide-brimmed hat.

h.Passport and travel papers (visa, if necessary) are essentials for travelling.

i.Electronic device charger and plug adaptor for use in Europe.

j.Charge your gadgets while you're on the road with a portable power bank.

K.Use a daypack or beach bag to transport your necessities on day excursions and activities.

l.First aid supplies and any prescription prescriptions you may need while travelling.

j.A compact first-aid kit that includes common items like bandages, painkillers, and antiseptic

k.Credit cards are frequently accepted, but it's still a good idea to carry some cash with you for minor transactions and in case you travel somewhere that doesn't take cards.

Remember to pack effectively and lightly since you may want to bring home some Lake Como trinkets. You'll be ready to take full advantage of your stay in Lake Como and its spectacular scenery and lovely environment if you follow our packing list.

CAR LEASES

Renting a vehicle gives you the freedom to explore other cities, sights, and hidden treasures at your own speed, making it a handy way to get to know Lake Como and its surroundings. What you should know about automobile rentals in the Lake Como area is as follows:

Rental Companies: Major cities like Como, Lecco, and other adjacent regions have a wide variety of automobile rental firms accessible. There are both international and regional vehicle rental businesses in the area, providing you a wide range of possibilities.

Booking in Advance: To guarantee availability and lock in the lowest prices, it's advised to reserve your rental vehicle in advance, particularly during busy travel times or on holidays.

Driving Permit: You must have a current driver's licence from your home country in order to hire a vehicle in Italy. You may also need an International Driving Permit (IDP) if the language of your driver's licence is either English or Italian.

Age Requirements: In Italy, drivers must be at least 21 years old to hire a vehicle, while certain companies may have a minimum age of 25.

Insurance: Standard insurance coverage is usually included in car rental costs. For added peace of mind, take into account supplemental insurance alternatives like Collision Damage Waiver (CDW) and Theft Protection (TP).

GPS and navigation: If your rental vehicle lacks an integrated GPS system, think about bringing your own or utilising a smartphone guidance software.

the ZTL Zones Pay attention to Zona a Traffico Limitato (ZTL) areas in several places. Residents only should access these restricted traffic zones, and doing so without the required authority may result in penalties. Keep an eye out for traffic signs at all times.

Parking: In busy tourist areas in particular, parking places may be scarce. When reserving your accommodations, be sure to ask about parking options. Some hotels provide parking services.

Driving in Italy: Acquaint yourself with the driving customs and regulations there. Keep an eye out for forceful Italian drivers, particularly in the bigger cities.

Fueling Up: There are several gas stations along main routes and highways. Credit cards are often accepted at stations, but it's a good idea to have extra cash on hand, particularly in remote locations.

Review the terms and conditions, including any extra costs, fuel rules, and drop-off guidelines, before confirming your auto hire. Renting a vehicle may give you the flexibility to explore Lake Como and the area around it, finding undiscovered attractions and taking pleasure in the gorgeous drives the area has to offer.

SOME DRIVING TIPS

Driving may be exhilarating and difficult while travelling. For a safe and happy driving experience, take into account the following advice if you want to drive in the Lake Como area or anyplace else in Italy:

IDP (International Driving Permit) Obtaining If your driver's licence is not in English or Italian, you need also get an International Driving Permit (IDP). Rental vehicle companies and authorities may ask for the IDP, which is a translation of your licence.

Become familiar with the local traffic laws: Learn the local driving laws and traffic regulations for Italy before you get behind the wheel. You may encounter restrictions that are different from your usual ones, such as those governing right-of-way and speed limits.

Maintain Speed Limits: Observe the speed limits, which are shown on signs in kilometres per hour (km/h). Typically, the posted speed limits are 50 km/h for towns, 90 km/h for rural routes, and 110–130 km/h for interstates.

Use Seatbelts: All passengers in the car, including those in the front and rear seats, must wear seat belts at all times.

Avoid ZTL Zones: ZTL Zones are limited traffic areas that may be found in certain cities and towns. If you don't have the required permission, avoid entering these zones since traffic cameras may automatically punish you.

The traffic in Italian cities may be crowded, and some of the drivers can be aggressive. Remain vigilant, often check your mirrors, and be wary of scooters and bicycles.

Understanding How to Use Roundabouts: In Italy, roundabouts are typical. Use your indicators to signify your departure and yield to any oncoming traffic as you enter the roundabout.

Avoid Rush Hours: If at all feasible, arrange your driving routes to avoid the busiest times of day for traffic in cities.

Parking: In crowded cities, parking may be difficult. To avoid penalties, look for authorised parking spots and observe any parking limitations.

Use hands-free devices: Unless you have a hands-free system, using a cell phone while driving is prohibited.

Watch for traffic signs: Pay close attention to traffic signs, particularly those indicating one-way streets, no-entry zones, and speed restrictions.

Be Wary of small Roads: Especially in ancient villages, some of the roads around Lake Como may be small. Take pedestrians into consideration while you drive carefully.

Enjoy the Scenic Drives: The scenic drives around Lake Como are beautiful. Take your time and enjoy the amazing vistas, stopping sometimes to take pictures of the splendour.

Exercise patience and care while driving abroad since it could vary from how you're accustomed to. Consider utilising public transit or hiring a local driver for certain excursions if you are uncomfortable driving in congested regions or on unfamiliar roads. Ultimately, keep your eyes on, drive safely, and enjoy the pleasure of driving around Lake Como.

Do's and Don'ts

Visitor guidelines for Lake Como and the area around it include the following:

Do's:

Respect Local Customs: Adopt the native way of life. The locals will welcome your use of simple Italian words and a "Buongiorno" or "Ciao" greeting.

Dress Appropriately: When attending upmarket restaurants or places of worship, dress modestly and avoid wearing beachwear.

Explore the Villages: The lovely towns around Lake Como are worth seeing since they each have their own special charms and attractions.

Enjoy the Cuisine: Savor the mouth watering Italian fare, which includes regional delicacies like risotto, spaghetti, and gelato.

Use Public Transportation: To explore the region and take in the views, think about using trains, boats, or ferries.

Plan Boat Trips: to see several cities and take in the beauty of Lake Como from the water.

Take pictures: Document the magnificent countryside, venerable buildings, and special moments while you're travelling.

Visit Gardens and Villas: Take some time to stroll among the lovely gardens and venerable homes like Villa Carlotta and Villa del Balbianello.

Enjoy Water Activities: On Lake Como's pristine waters, swim, sail, or engage in other water sports.

Enjoy Local Festivals: If your visit falls during one of the area's many festivals or events, take advantage of the chance to get a taste of the rich culture of the area.

Don'ts:

Don't Rush: Avoid hurrying from one site to the next; Lake Como is a place to unwind and take in the scenery.

Don't Ignore ZTL Zones: Be aware of restricted traffic zones (ZTL) in certain places and stay clear of them unless you have permission to be there.

Avoid Tipping Too Much: Although it is customary to offer a little gratuity for exceptional service, excessive tipping is not accepted in Italy.

Don't Disregard Parking restrictions: Follow parking restrictions to prevent tickets or towing.

Don't Swim in Restricted Areas: Follow safety precautions and refrain from swimming in places marked with warning signs or where it is forbidden.

Don't Hesitate to Ask For Help:If you want assistance or instructions, don't be afraid to approach locals or seek assistance at tourist information offices.

Don't Forget Cash: Despite the widespread use of credit cards, have some cash on hand for minor transactions or in locations where cards aren't accepted.

Don't Litter: Respect the environment and properly dispose of rubbish by not littering. Keep Lake Como's lovely surroundings spotless.

Don't Overpack: If you want to visit many places and use public transit, pack less.

Don't Skip the Scenic Drives: Take advantage of the stunning scenery and unforgettable experiences that the scenic drives surrounding Lake Como have to offer.

By abiding by these dos and don'ts, you can make sure that your vacation to Lake Como is courteous and pleasurable while also maximising its stunning scenery, extensive culture, and welcoming people.

Travel Insurance

Any journey, including your trip to Lake Como, must have travel insurance. In the event that unanticipated circumstances arise that could interfere with your trip plans or result in unforeseen costs, it offers financial security and peace of mind. Consider the following important factors when buying travel insurance:

Coverage: Travel insurance often provides coverage for a variety of trip-related occurrences, including trip interruptions or cancellations, medical crises, lost or delayed luggage, and travel delays.

Medical Emergencies: Travel insurance should cover hospitalisation, medical care, and, if required, medical evacuation in the event of a medical emergency.

Trip Cancellations and Interruptions: This insurance covers you in the event that you have to postpone or cancel your trip owing to one of the specified situations, such as sickness, accident, or unforeseeable circumstances.

Baggage and Personal Property: Loss, theft, or damage to your baggage and personal property should be covered by your travel insurance.

Travel Delays: If you have delays or miss a connection, your insurance may cover the extra costs.

Pre-existing Medical Condition: whether you have any pre-existing medical issues, find out whether the insurance covers them or if you need to get extra coverage.

Activities and Adventure Sports: Verify that your insurance policy covers any activities or adventure sports you want to participate in.

Policy Exclusions: Carefully read the exclusions in the policy to understand what is not covered. Reckless conduct, unreported pre-existing conditions, or engaging in high-risk activities are examples of frequent exclusions.

Travel Duration: Verify that the insurance coverage covers the whole journey, from the time of departure to the time of arrival.

Compare Policies: Comparing plans can help you choose the one that best meets your requirements and offers sufficient coverage for your trip.

Emergency Assistance: Determine if the insurance provider has helplines you may contact in an emergency and 24-hour emergency support.

To assure dependability and excellent customer service, check reviews and ratings of the insurance company before getting travel insurance.

To obtain the most coverage, it is advised to buy travel insurance as soon as you arrange your trip. Read the policy paperwork thoroughly, understand the terms and conditions, and if you have any questions, contact the insurance company. If you have travel insurance, you can relax and enjoy your vacation to Lake Como knowing that you are covered in case anything unexpected happens.

Responsible Travel Practices

Responsible travel practices, usually referred to as sustainable or ethical travel, entail making decisions that maximise the advantages to the places you visit while minimising any negative effects on the environment, culture, or community. In order to travel responsibly, keep the following in mind when visiting Lake Como:

Respect Local Culture and Customs: Learn about the regional traditions, customs, and culture of Lake Como, and show respect by abiding by them while you are there.

Support Local Businesses: Make the decision to patronise neighbourhood eateries, stores, and lodging facilities since doing so boosts the local economy and improves the neighbourhood.

Reduce Plastic Usage: Say no to plastic straws and bags and carry a reusable water bottle and shopping bag to help reduce the usage of single-use plastics.

Conserve Water and Energy: Water and energy conservation are important, particularly in areas where resources are perhaps limited or in high demand.

Choose Eco-Friendly Accommodations: Opt for eco-friendly lodgings that follow sustainable principles, such reducing trash and conserving energy.

Utilise Public transit or Carpool: To cut down on carbon emissions and traffic congestion, utilise public transit or carpool wherever feasible.

Respect Wildlife: Take pleasure in Lake Como's unspoiled beauty without endangering the local fauna or their habitats. Avert feeding wild animals and any other activity that can endanger them.

Leave No Trace: Keep Lake Como clean by properly disposing of garbage and other litter, and refrain from leaving any trash or personal items behind.

Support Conservation Effort: Think about going to your neighbourhood nature preserve or conservation group and giving them your support.

Be Mindful of Water Activities: Be careful not to damage the water or disrupt aquatic life while engaging in water activities like boating or swimming.

Engage in Responsible Photography: Practising responsible photography is being mindful while shooting pictures, particularly of people and holy places. Always get the go-ahead before taking pictures of locals.

Respect Wildlife Sanctuaries and Protected Areas: To maintain the preservation of natural environments, follow the laws and regulations in wildlife sanctuaries and protected areas.

Give Back: Consider giving back to the neighbourhood by taking part in projects for responsible tourism or volunteering with neighbourhood groups.

Learn Responsible Travel Practices: To encourage sustainable tourism, educate yourself on responsible travel methods. Then, share your information with other tourists.

You can help save Lake Como's natural splendour and cultural history and ensure that future generations may continue to enjoy this gorgeous location by adhering to these responsible travel guidelines.

TOP TOURIST DESTINATION

One of the most popular tourist attractions in both Italy and Europe, Lake Como is known for its magnificent natural beauty, quaint villages, important historical sites, and opulent lakeside lifestyle. The following are some of the most popular tourist sites and places around Lake Como:

Bellagio: Often referred to as the "Pearl of Lake Como," Bellagio is a charming town with breathtaking vistas, opulent homes, and lovely gardens like Villa Melzi.

Varenna: Varenna is a charming, picturesque town with colourful homes, winding cobblestone lanes, and the old Villa Monastero.

Como: The largest city on Lake Como, Como has a bustling downtown area, a stunning cathedral, and a funicular that takes visitors to Brunate for sweeping views.

Villa del Balbianello: A beautiful terraced garden and historical home with stunning lake views are located on a peninsula. Additionally, it's a well-liked site for shooting movies like "Star Wars."

Tremezzo: The opulent Villa Carlotta, renowned for its art collection and verdant botanical gardens, is located here.

Menaggio: is a quaint lakeside community with a picturesque promenade, old-world architecture, and convenient access to the mountains beyond.

Isola Comacina: The lone island in Lake Como, Isola Comacina, provides a calm atmosphere, a few dining options, and historical relics.

Como-Brunate Funicular: offers breathtaking panoramic views of Lake Como and the surrounding mountains as it travels from Como to Brunate.

Piona Abbey: is a serene Benedictine monastery with a lake view that is well-known for its historical and artistic value.

Silk Museum of Como: Learn about the history of silk manufacture in Lake Como at the Silk Museum of Como and be inspired by the craftsmanship involved.

Forte Montecchio Nord: Discover the history of World War I at this old fort.

Villa Olmo: is a neoclassical Como home with lovely grounds that often hosts cultural events and exhibits.

Lido di Lenno: is a lakeside beach and pool complex that is perfect for swimming and relaxing.

Orrido di Bellano: A stunning natural canyon with trails and waterfalls that makes for an exhilarating outdoor adventure.

Villa Monastero in Varenna: Discover the opulent Villa Monastero in Varenna, complete with a botanical garden that overlooks the lake.

Due to its unrivalled beauty, rich cultural history, and plenty of outdoor activities, Lake Como is a popular vacation spot for those looking for both adventure and leisure. None of your interests—history, nature, or just taking in the peace and quiet—Lake Como has a multitude of activities that will dazzle you and have you coming back for more.

ORGANISED TOURS AND PRIVATE GUIDES

Private guides and organised excursions may add value, convenience, and individualised attention to your time at Lake Como. What you need know about both choices is as follows:

Organized Tours:

Types of Tours: There are many different types of organised excursions available around Lake Como, including boat tours, walking tours, sightseeing tours, cuisine tours, and more. They often provide pre-planned itineraries and cover well-known destinations.

Group Tours: You may explore Lake Como with other tourists on a group excursion. They are often guided by competent tour leaders who impart valuable information and local history.

Convenience: Because organized tours handle logistics, transportation, and admittance costs, they are convenient. You may just sign up for the trip and concentrate on having fun.

Itineraries that have already been planned: Tours are created with predetermined itineraries so you can visit the highlights and don't have to bother about organising the finer details.

Social Aspect: Group trips provide you the chance to socialize and exchange stories with other tourists.

Private Guides:

Personalized Experience: By hiring a private guide, you may tailor your itinerary to your interests and preferences. You have greater freedom to decide where you want to go and how long you want to stay there.

In-Depth Knowledge: Locals or specialists with extensive knowledge of the history, culture, and secret attractions of Lake Como often serve as private guides.

Skip the Line: By hiring a private guide, you may be able to avoid waiting in line for popular sights, maximising your experience and saving time.

One-on-One Attention: You get individualized attention and may enquire about the locations you go to.

Customized speed: Private tour guides may go at your speed to make sure you have a relaxing and pleasurable day.

Choosing Between Tours and Private Guides

a.Organized tours might be a fantastic alternative if you value convenience and meeting new people.

b.A private guide can be your best option if you want a more specialized and in-depth experience.

c.When comparing tour possibilities, take into account the size of the group, the guide's level of experience, and the activities offered.

Whether you choose public tours or private guides, both may make your trip to Lake Como more memorable by providing insightful information. In the end, everything comes down to your choices and travel habits.

Photography Rules

It's important to respect surroundings, privacy, and local traditions while shooting pictures at Lake Como. Keep in mind the following photographic restrictions and regulations:

Respect privacy: When photographing portraits or up-close pictures of individuals, you should always get their consent. It's possible that some people don't feel comfortable having their images taken.

Respect "No Photography" Signs or limitations: Be aware of any "No Photography" signs or limitations at private, public, or religious locations.

Be Conscious of Others: When shooting pictures in busy places, avoid blocking walkways or interfering with other people's pleasure.

Protect the environment: by shooting pictures without causing any harm to historical or natural locations. Avoid walking on plants, handling fragile objects, and leaving any trash behind.

Use Drones With Permission: If you want to use a drone for aerial photography, be careful to abide by local laws and secure any required licences or approvals.

Respect Local traditions: Pay attention to regional sensibilities and traditions, particularly during holidays or religious occasions.

Be Discreet: It's ideal to take pictures quietly and without disturbing others while taking pictures at ceremonies or private gatherings, for example.

post Photos Sensibly: If you want to post your images on websites or social media, be sure they are considerate and don't violate anyone's privacy.

Don't Overuse Flash: Using flash may be forbidden in certain interior spaces, such as museums, to safeguard artwork or antiques.

Be Patient and Observant: Give yourself plenty of time to examine your surroundings and record unscripted moments that highlight Lake Como's natural beauty and genuineness.

The beauty of Lake Como may be captured via photography, but it's important to practise respect and consideration at all times. You may assure a pleasant and courteous photographic experience when visiting by adhering to these guidelines.

Night life

Although some of its villages have a lively nightlife, Lake Como is most recognized for its tranquil and scenic daylight scenery. Even while it may not have as vibrant a nightlife as bigger cities like Milan, there are still plenty of interesting things to do in the evenings. Here are some choices for enjoying Lake Como's nightlife:

Bars & Pubs: There are several villages around Lake Como that feature bars and pubs where you can unwind and mingle with residents and tourists. Drink in the view of the lake or the bustling streets of the town while sipping on a drink or glass of wine.

Lakeside Restaurants: Some restaurants by the lake provide a romantic and serene ambiance in the evenings where you may enjoy delectable Italian food while admiring the moonlight lake.

Live Music: It's possible to locate pubs or other places in certain cities where local bands, jazz, or acoustic sessions play live. Look into any concerts or events taking place while you are there.

Cultural Events: On occasion, Lake Como offers cultural events like outdoor concerts, theatrical productions, or movie showings. Watch the local event calendar to see what's going on while you're there.

Casinò di Campione d'Italia: The renowned Casino di Campione d'Italia is a short drive from Lake Como and is a great place to go if you like gaming and entertainment.

Evening Boat Cruises: Several tour companies provide evening boat tours on Lake Como so that you may take in the breathtaking view while the stars shine.

Night time Strolls: Take leisurely strolls along the lakefront boulevards or explore the lit historic districts of cities like Como and Bellagio at night.

It's crucial to remember that Lake Como is recognized for its tranquil atmosphere and that there may not be as much nighttime activity there as there is in bigger towns. But in the evenings, it offers the ideal chance to unwind, take in the splendour of the lake, and take in the local culture at a more leisurely pace.

Insider Advice for First Timers

Here are some insider tips for visitors to Lake Como for the first time to help you get the most out of your visit:

Explore Several Towns: The picturesque villages that surround Lake Como, each with its own distinct personality, should be explored. To appreciate the varied beauties of the area, tour many towns like Bellagio, Varenna, and Menaggio rather than sticking to just one.

Take a Boat Tour: Viewing Lake Como from the boat is one of the greatest ways to appreciate its beauty. To see breath-taking views of the lake and its surroundings, think about going on a boat excursion.

Visit Lake Como in the Shoulder Seasons: Although Lake Como is stunning all year round, you may want to go there in the spring or fall when it's less crowded and the weather is still lovely.

Plan day trips: Use Milan, Lugano (Switzerland), and the Italian Alps as a starting point for your excursions away from Lake Como. These days, excursions provide your schedule variety.

Sample Local Cuisine: The area around Lake Como provides several great cuisines. Indulge in gelato while trying regional delicacies including risotto, pizzoccheri, and freshwater fish.

Take the Funicular to Brunate: for Panoramic Views of the Lake and Surrounding Mountains. Board the Como-Brunate Funicular. The trip itself is an adventure.

Discover Hidden Gems: Lake Como offers a lot of off-the-beaten-path hidden jewels. For a more personal experience, explore lesser-known towns, overlooks, and walking paths.

Pack Comfortable Shoes: The landscape around Lake Como may be rough and uneven, particularly in the villages, so bring comfortable shoes. To comfortably tour the region, you must wear shoes that are comfortable for walking.

Embrace the Slow Pace: Lake Como is a tranquil setting where you may unwind. Enjoy the relaxed environment, the leisurely pace, and the moments.

Learn Basic phrases: While many residents are English speakers, learning a few basic Italian words can improve your relationships and demonstrate respect for the local way of life.

Respect the Environment: Lake Como's clean surroundings are essential to maintaining its beauty. Be responsible, refrain from littering, and support environmentally beneficial actions.

Capture the Beauty: Lake Como provides endless options for shooting beautiful images, whether you're a professional photographer or just want to take pictures for fun. Remember to bring your camera!

You may have a memorable and satisfying experience on your first trip to the magnificent Lake Como area by heeding these insider suggestions. Enjoy this Italian treasure's breathtaking scenery, vibrant culture, and welcoming people.

FOND FAREWELL: LEAVING LAKE COMO WITH CHERISHED MEMORIES

Even while leaving Lake Como after an incredible trip might be difficult, you'll always treasure the beautiful scenery, rich culture, and kind people you encountered there. Here are some ideas to help you bid Lake Como a loving goodbye as you leave:

Capture last moments: Before you go, spend some time capturing Lake Como's splendour in pictures or sketching. These souvenirs will be enduring keepsakes of your amazing experience.

Visit a Special Spot: Return to a favourite location near the lake for one last period of peace and contemplation. Say your goodbyes while being appreciative of the memories you've built, whether you're at a picturesque vantage point, a lakeside promenade, or a quaint town square.

Buy Souvenirs: By bringing treasured mementos home, you may take a piece of Lake Como with you. Beautiful postcards, handcrafted goods, and locally produced crafts may all make excellent souvenirs.

Share Your Experience: Share pictures, tales, and experiences from your Lake Como excursion with loved ones. Your adventures could encourage others to visit this magical place.

Express Gratitude: Thank the people and organisations who helped make your vacation special if you experienced remarkable hospitality or compassion while visiting.

Recall Specific Events: Think back on the interactions you had and the memories you created while visiting Lake Como. Keep in mind the wonderful dinners, beautiful sunsets, and laughing you shared.

Promise to Come Back: Say "arrivederci" (goodbye) to Lake Como and make a future trip commitment. The eternal beauty of Lake Como will always be there, ready for your next trip.

Write In your travel journal: Consider keeping a trip notebook where you may record your most cherished ideas, experiences, and comments. You'll be able to revisit the experiences in the future thanks to this personal record.

Keep in Touch: If you made friends while there, give them your contact information so you may keep in touch and maintain the relationships you formed there.

Embrace the Journey: Take in the travel ahead and the great memories you've made as you leave from Lake Como. Bring the spirit of Lake Como with you and use it to motivate your future explorations.

As you bid Lake Como farewell, take a minute to think back on the magical adventures you've had and the precious times you've spent with loved ones. Keep in mind that Lake Como's beauty and charm will always be a part of you, and that the memories you make there will make you nostalgic and happy in the years to come. Arrivederci, Lake Como, till we meet again!

Last-Minute Gifts and Souvenirs

Don't worry if you just have a little amount of time left before leaving Lake Como but still want to pick up a few last-minute presents and keepsakes. There are several practical choices available. Here are some suggestions for last-minute Lake Como gifts and souvenirs:

Local Food and Wine: Pick up some regional treats like handcrafted chocolates, classic cookies, or a bottle of Italian wine. These are simple to acquire in nearby stores and make excellent presents.

Souvenir Store: Visit the gift stores in well-known tourist destinations including Bellagio, Como, and Varenna. There are many different souvenirs available, including keychains, magnets, postcards, and t-shirts.

Crafts and Artwork manufactured by Local Artists: Look for locally manufactured crafts and artwork. These one-of-a-kind items, which range from paintings to ceramics, offer thoughtful and memorable presents.

Local Olive Oil or Balsamic Vinegar: Get a bottle of premium local olive oil or balsamic vinegar to give as a present to food-loving friends or to add an authentic Italian touch to your kitchen.

Fashion Accessories: Look for jewellery, leather items, and scarves at boutique stores that feature Italian design and workmanship.

Locally Made Cosmetics & Soaps: Lake Como is renowned for crafting wonderful cosmetics and soaps from all-natural components. These things are excellent presents for loved ones and friends.

Photographic Prints: If you captured beautiful images of Lake Como while you were there, think about printing and framing them as unique keepsakes or presents.

Local Artisan products: Look for locally produced goods, such as scarves or ties made of Como silk, which are recognized for their high quality and workmanship.

Handwritten Postcards: As a lovely surprise for loved ones, write emotional sentiments on handwritten postcards depicting the beautiful views of Lake Como.

Culinary Kits: Some stores provide kits that enable customers to make Italian foods at home, such as sets for making pasta or pizza.

Always keep in mind that the message behind the present is what is really important, and even little, sentimental trinkets may capture the soul of your Lake Como vacation. You may locate beautiful presents and mementos to give to loved ones and cherish as enduring reminders of your stay at Lake Como with a little imagination and investigation.

Reflecting on Your Lake Como Experience

A lovely method to recall the magical moments and feelings that the location created is to go back on your time spent at Lake Como. Here are some reflection-sparking questions to consider:

Serene Beauty: During your trip to Lake Como, what were some of the most beautiful sights and tranquil settings you saw?

Cultural Immersion: How did you get fully absorbed in the traditions and culture of the area? What special encounters did you have that allowed you to get a glimpse of Lake Como's true character?

Memorable Moments: Think back on the experiences that will always stick with you, whether it was a stunning sunset, a delicious dinner, or a heartfelt interaction with a local.

Favourite Activities: What were some of your favourite Lake Como-area activities? What made these experiences unique, whether it was a boat trip on the lake, a beautiful trek, or seeing quaint villages?

Culinary Delight: Describe the tastes and flavours of the regional food you sampled. Have you tried any new foods or substances that have made an impression on your palate?

Connection with Nature: How did you interact with nature when you were in Lake Como? Did you go hiking in the nearby mountains, go swimming in the pristine waterways, or just enjoy the beauty of the natural surroundings?

Timeless Charm: Which facets of Lake Como's classic beauty and charm captured your attention the most? What emotions were evoked by the area's atmosphere?

Getting Along with the Locals: Talk about your encounters with the locals. Did you have talks with them that revealed details about their way of life?

Personal Growth: Consider any personal development or fresh viewpoints you may have acquired throughout your journey to Lake Como. Has the event affected you long-term?

Future Dreams: Do you have any ideas or aspirations including travel, discovery, or interacting with the environment and culture after your trip to Lake Como?

You may absorb the beauty of your trip and recognize the moments that made it memorable by thinking back on your time at Lake Como. Additionally, it helps you to keep Lake Como's spirit with you, cherishing the experiences and applying the principles you learnt to your everyday life. As you reflect on your time spent at Lake Como, keep in mind that the place's charm will always be a part of you, waiting to be rediscovered anytime you need a dose of its tranquil appeal.

Made in the USA
Middletown, DE
04 September 2023

37962989R00144